Integrating Services for Children and Families

Integrating Services for Children and Families

Understanding the Past to Shape the Future

Sharon Lynn Kagan

with Peter R. Neville

Yale University Press
New Haven & London

Published in cooperation
with the National Center
for Service Integration

Published with assistance from the
Louis Stern Memorial Fund.

This document was written pursuant to a grant from the U.S.
Department of Health and Human Services. The opinions
and conclusions expressed herein are solely those of the
authors and should not be construed as representing the
opinions or policy of any agency of the Federal Government.

Set in Sabon text and Gill Sans Condensed display type by
Keystone Typesetting, Inc., Orwigsburg, Pennsylvania.

Printed in the United States of America by
Vail-Ballou Press, Binghamton, New York.

Library of Congress Cataloging-in-Publication Data
Kagan, Sharon Lynn.
Integrating services for children and families : understanding the
past to shape the future / Sharon Lynn Kagan with Peter Neville.
p. cm.
"Published in cooperation with the National Center for
Service Integration."
Includes bibliographical references and index.
ISBN 0-300-05871-3 (alk. paper)
1. Social service—United States. 2. Social work
administration—United States. I. Neville, Peter. II. Title.
HV95.K278   1994
361.973—dc20   93-31023
CIP

A catalogue record for this book is available
from the British Library.

The paper in this book meets the guidelines for permanence
and durability of the Committee on Production Guidelines
for Book Longevity of the Council on Library Resources.

10 9 8 7 6 5 4 3 2 1

To the pioneers of service integration, who challenged
the status quo, combatted complacency, and kept their
focus on the human element of human services.

Contents

Preface

Philosophers have only interpreted the world in different ways. The point, however, is to change it.—Hegel

In reviewing the history of service integration, one is struck by its nobility of intent, its tenacity of purpose, and the ineffectiveness of its implementation. Why these efforts—so well-intentioned and so purposeful—have met with only isolated triumphs and have had only marginal impact on service delivery is both puzzling and instructive. The aim of this book is to extract lessons from this enigmatic history that may be helpful in planning future reforms and in redirecting current trends in the delivery of social services.

The literature on service integration is at once abundant and sparse, depending on how one defines the term. If one limits *service integration* to mean the integration of social services, the literature consists only of several major analytic reviews, qualitative studies, and reports. Conversely, if one broadens the definition to include organizational theory, intergovernmental relations, institutional change, categorical approaches, and specific strategies (such as case management and collocation), the literature is extensive indeed. This book attempts to strike a balance between the two. On the one hand, it recognizes that close attention must be paid to those writings that take the limited view of service integration. On the other hand, it acknowledges that, like service integration itself, this study would be severely hampered if it did not take other related literatures into consideration. Consequently, while focusing on service integration, it brings together theoretical work and practical lessons from allied domains.

Part I is a historical review of service integration. Chapter 1 examines the sociopolitical antecedents of service integration that have emerged from the uniquely democratic experience of the United States. Chapters 2 and 3 analyze formal attempts at service integration and stress the cacophony of broad-based multidisciplinary efforts of the early 1970s, with special emphasis on research and development and on policy initiatives. Chapter 4 concludes the section by addressing the comparatively recent and more circumscribed categorical approaches to service integration.

Part II presents the theoretical context for emerging ideas about service integration. Chapter 5 examines evolving and remarkably diverse definitions of service integration. Chapter 6 explicates differing theoretical approaches—structuralist, humanistic, and systemic—that have undergirded and given rise to different definitions, conceptualizations, and approaches to service integration.

Turning from theory to action, Part III extracts lessons from the past that directly inform practice. Chapter 7 delineates action frameworks or typologies that codify approaches to service integration. Chapter 8 presents the barriers to and incentives for implementation, and chapter 9 discusses specific activities that compose the repertoire of service integration strategies. The book concludes (Part IV) with a discussion of the implications of this analysis (chapter 10) and reasonable recommendations for future work on service integration (chapter 11).

In the preparation of this book, I am indebted to the heroic work of those who have trod the scientific and practical path before. Their efforts have been herculean, but have not always produced immediate benefit or garnered tangible results. Therefore, this work is dedicated to them for trailblazing very rough terrain. I am grateful to Project SHARE, a national clearinghouse founded in the mid-1970s to help improve the management of human services, for providing me with a rich reservoir of resources. In addition, the wealth of information and documents collected by James Dolson, heretofore unavailable publicly, have enabled me to examine the most fertile period of federal service integration in considerable depth. I am indebted to Richard Silva, Terry Bond, and Carole Oshinsky for their tenacity in accessing these materials. I also wish to thank the U.S. Department of Health and Human Services for its financial support and for its longtime commitment to service integration. Yale University and the Bush Center in Child Development and Social Policy have given me the intellectual forum for this investigation and the liberty to integrate those avenues of action and inquiry that I believe are crucial to improving the life chances of children and families and, ultimately, repairing the social fabric of the nation. I am most indebted to my wonderful colleagues at the National Center for Service Integration, and to Sidney Gardner, Martin Gerry, and William Morrill, whose early review meaningfully contributed to this book. I wish especially to thank Peter Neville, who assisted with the research for this work and wrote chapter 9.

Sharon L. Kagan
New Haven, Conn.
September 1993

Part I

Service Integration in Historical Perspective

1

Sociopolitical Antecedents

The inception of American service integration is often dated to the late 1960s, when, to be sure, an abundance of activity took hold. Such dating, however, ignores critical antecedents in American sociopolitical history that created the context and need for service integration. Similarly, it ignores important efforts—though not dubbed *service integration* per se—that did integrate social services. Therefore, this book begins by looking back at an earlier point in history and taking into account an array of historical forces that set the stage for service integration efforts from the 1960s to the present.

The Colonial Period

Because the history of service integration is inextricably meshed with notions of both federalism and

3

the human service obligations of a government to its citizens, its origins can be traced to the very origins of our nation. Service integration is rooted in the American colonial experience and the arrival of the first immigrants—a quarter of a million by 1700. Amid these were many who arrived as a result of British deportation policies that purged undesirables—vagrants, felons, and the poor—from the motherland. America became home to these individuals, who congregated in seaport towns, seeking opportunities in the land that promised so much to so many.

In these early days, the embryonic social service structure began to take shape. Not unexpectedly, it bore the clear mark of English traditions (Lynn 1980). Using the Poor Law of 1601 as a model, towns and parishes provided relief when informal supports—families and friends—were unavailable or unable to respond. In so doing, precedent for community intervention was established; communities intervened when other supports failed. Moreover, categories of need were defined so that community residence was a condition of eligibility. As demands on community resources soared, towns turned to the colonial governments, pressing them into the role of tertiary service providers. The colonies provided relief to those who could not establish residence in a given town and those unable to be attended by family or community.

With the colony as the provider of last resort, demands on towns for poor support increased. In the face of mounting population growth, frequent epidemics and wars, rising immigration, and a diminishing focus on charity, community attitudes toward the poor gradually deteriorated. Those who were once seen as essentially virtuous but without means came to be regarded as idle paupers laden with vice and destructive to the new society. As the numbers of transient and unemployed poor grew, so did the stigma attached to their dependence.

The New Republic and Its Conceptions of Public Responsibility

Undergirding these constructions of social policy lay a profound operational ambivalence regarding the role of society in service to the poor.

Though considered the responsibility of kith and kin first, the poor were increasing in numbers and by the time of the founding of the United States constituted a growing challenge to the republic. Avoiding all support courted social catastrophe; alternatively, serving the poor fully yielded immediate economic strains and contradicted the moral intent of the new nation. Finding a balance between avoiding and assuming full responsibility for the destitute, the United States turned to the volunteer sector—religious institutions in particular—to render support, at once reinforcing the ambivalence of the colonial era and predicting that of eras to come.

Such a solution was both supported and complicated by another factor: the intentional federalist duality. From the earliest days of the republic, champions of states' rights clashed with champions of more centralized federal power, raising the issue of which level of government should be responsible in which ways for the indigent. Ideological differences divided President George Washington's administration: Thomas Jefferson, the secretary of state, favored state authority and Alexander Hamilton, the secretary of the treasury, advocated national authority. With the Constitution specifying no clear direction, political leaders of each era have been left to chart an instrumental view of federalism, one that allows for malleability dependent on the policy aims of the era. This flexibility, begun early in the national history, has been perpetuated, with periodic fluctuations in attitudes toward and support for the welfare state. With neither consistent commitment nor a clearly delineated pattern of social obligation, America has lacked both a definite agent and an objective for social services, leading Rein (1970) to note, "A good case could be made for viewing social services as a psychedelic mosaic—where the boundaries are vague, overlapping and uncertain [, and] reality and myth merge" (p. 104).

The lack of clearly assigned roles and of a coordinated strategy of social provision in the early days of the republic should not be equated with inefficiency. Support for the indigent was regarded as more a local responsibility, and the needs of the poor were met through a variety of supports, including local magistrates, bureaucrats, the church, and the family. The state was tacitly entrusted with a secondary support role, and engagement on the federal level was quite limited. Operating fairly efficiently, the unintegrated system prevailed until it became functionally immobilized by the inundation of disease, unemployment, poverty, and other stresses on the community. As in the colonial era, public sentiment interpreted such circumstances as signals of a decaying morality.

To combat the escalating problem, states began authorizing towns, cities, and municipalities to assume an even greater role via the establishment of almshouses, poor farms, and asylums. Designed both to segregate and to rehabilitate the poor, these institutions—though derived from the public concern of primarily lay reformers—soon were being run by professionals. In 1844, for example, the Association of Medical Superintendents of American Institutions for the Insane was formed to advance the cause. As institutions became professionalized, they lost their reform spirit and increasingly became dumping grounds for societal outcasts. Additionally, needs began to be defined more precisely, with specialized interest groups—some of them largely composed of professionals—advocating narrowly defined services targeted to specific groups. Children, widows, paupers, the mentally ill, and criminals began to be viewed as distinct populations with different needs that required specialized forms of treatment and custody.

The Civil War and Its Aftermath

Just as the Civil War was a turning point in so much of American life, it spearheaded a shift in ideology toward greater sympathy and support for the human services. Following the war, emancipated slaves, orphaned children, and displaced families confronted states and local communities with an increased need for housing, food, and medical support. This need was further exacerbated by continued immigration and accelerated industrialization. Human services institutions, despite their ambiguity of auspices and lack of accountability, were strongly supported, in part because they fulfilled a sense of social obligation and in part because they served as effective vehicles for controlling and segregating the deviant and dependent.

Recognizing the growing internal problems that such institutions faced—problems later eloquently detailed in Rothman's *The Discovery of the Asylum* (1971)—states set up oversight boards to advise institutions and legislatures. Some recommended greater efficiency through the centralization of services at the front line, while others sounded calls for the integration of administrative welfare functions. The period between the end of the war and the turn of the century is also notable because "contemporary themes and tensions surfaced in legislative deliberations over state aid to the needy: coordination, economy, professionalization, specialization, centralization, and integration" (Lynn 1980, p. 21).

Not surprisingly, inventive America, historically suspicious of government intervention, turned to the private sector. From Reconstruction through World War I, the human services landscape was marked by the emergence of private charities and mutual aid societies. At first, evangelical and philanthropic groups coalesced in small numbers. Soon, however, many organizations emerged, fueled by the development of an upper class and by the desire of well-to-do women who were eager to compensate for their growing economic separation from the poor.

Another product of the era, settlement houses, took hold, with the first opening in New York in 1886, followed quickly by Hull House in Chicago. Settlement houses, designed to counter the impersonalization of charity organizations and large institutions (Addams [1910] 1972), were more intimate, community-based, and comprehensive in orientation. Indeed, it was the community orientation of the settlement houses that provided the key to their success (Brueckner 1963). Weissbourd (1987) notes that community social ills of all sorts became targets of action. The settlement houses encouraged advocacy work and focused on holistic goals of bettering the environment for families. Though some settlement houses began by seeking to provide a single service, many soon dispensed with this strategy, recognizing that it underutilized their potential. Ultimately, settlement houses became vehicles for community mobilization as well as pioneers of the concept of multiple-service organizations.

But all was not rosy. While integrating services, settlement houses extended many of the assumptions that were shaping human service delivery. Specifically, the use of a service came to be seen—perhaps too optimistically—as a vehicle to reform deep-seated economic and social problems that transcended the neighborhood. Moreover, a tacit assumption of family hopelessness and inadequacy undergirded service delivery (Halpern 1991).

Despite these issues, services to the poor and indigent burgeoned both during and after Reconstruction. As early as 1878, Philadelphia, for example, had more than eight hundred service groups. The work of these many organizations needed to be coordinated. In 1877, the Charity Organization Societies (cos) were established, as Bush (1988) notes, to bring order to an overlapping and uncoordinated set of charities. The cos focused primarily on private charities and stressed that indigent behavior was fueled by faulty community organization—a sentiment that acknowledged the need to coordinate and integrate human services.

Historical interpretations of the rationale for the cos differ widely. Some suggest that their development was associated with the spirit of altruism that characterized the era. This was a time when well-intentioned and well-to-do women went into the homes of the indigent, attempting to rescue them from poverty. A second rationale for the establishment of the cos was more ameliorative. Rooted in the worsening economic conditions of the poor and the simultaneous expansion of the corporate economy, there was recognition of a growing and potentially dangerous schism between rich and poor. The cos were regarded as one vehicle to expedite services and therefore to help reduce the income gap and concomitant social strife. Reflecting the intensity of the problem, Katz (1981; cited in Halpern, 1991) notes that the poor were both the products and the casualties of capitalism. The cos therefore emerged as one of society's responses to assuage the negative consequences of poverty and fragmentation.

A third rationale, neither altruistic or ameliorative, was clearly economic. Simultaneous to the growth of those concerned about the obligations of a society to its poor were growing numbers who were concerned that overabundant charity would serve as a disincentive to gainful employment. This argument, taken to an extreme, asserted that too liberal a policy would undermine a thriving economic system by enticing workers out of the employment stream. Charity, particularly if it was uncoordinated and abundant, would destroy self-reliance, inhibit initiative, and further weaken the moral character of already corrupted paupers. The COS therefore had the moral responsibility to eradicate duplication of services and, more important, duplication of cash payments to the poor.

The legacies of the COS experience are central to an understanding of the evolution of professional social work and American service integration. First, the COS hastened the development of professionalism in that the women who advised the indigent, at first in a volunteer capacity, recognized that they needed specialized training in order to be effective in their work with the poor. This formed a basis for the evolution of schools of social work and the bedrock for much of the spirit of professionalism that evolved in social service fields.

Second, the rationales for much of the service integration work that was to follow surfaced in the COS experience. Briar (1982) has noted that the service integration movement has two primary roots, "one concerned with efficiency, reduction of duplication and administrative flexibility and the other reflecting a desire to maximize the ease and effectiveness with which multiple services can be delivered to the same client" (p. 117). Certainly the former rationale characterized the COS's work, and one might suspect that this intense interest in organizational reform led to similarly close attention to service delivery.

Third, though the intent of the COS was to coordinate services, in retrospect it seemed to add to their fragmentation. The class-based COS movement, with its concern primarily for private activities, came to focus on populations that *could* be saved from pauperism and rehabilitated. Those deemed irredeemable were referred to public institutions, further reinforcing the notion that such institutions were warehouses for the hopeless and that the state was the provider of last resort. The ultimate result of these early efforts was the more-than-semantic division of labor between "relief in the public sector and charity in the private sector" (Rein 1970, p. 109).

Increased professionalization and the Progressive movement ushered in ideological changes. Rather than regarding the government as the provider of last resort, Progressives envisioned the federal government's role as the protector of the distressed and the guarantor of individual opportunity and equity. Rather than blaming the individual, they tended to contextualize the problems, attributing them to broader social forces. The solutions varied as well. Instead of shunting off the indigent to institutions for societal relief, Progressives chose to attack root causes of poverty and advocated social insurance and social supports for the aged and widows with dependent children.

Fueled by the energy of the settlement house workers, these activities led to action at the federal level of government in the form of the first White House Conference on Children in 1909 and the 1912 congressional authorization of the Children's Bureau. The Shepard-Towner Act of 1921—though opposed by many of the private charities and allowed to lapse in 1929—authorized federal matching grants to states to reduce infant mortality. Well before the Social Security Act of 1935, the states assumed new roles in human service delivery, with attention given to categorical programs. The federal government began to be viewed as a catalyst for change through information dissemination and categorical grants.

The 1930s, 1940s, and 1950s

The devastating effects of the Great Depression forced America to realize what Europe had already acknowledged, that some form of temporary relief and social insurance was necessary. Although early reformers distinguished between social *insurance* programs (compulsory, government-managed self-help) and social *welfare* programs (government-managed charity), it was clear that the states were not equipped to provide such supports alone. Building upon the Progressive agenda, the federal government created numerous relief programs, not only stimulating state agencies to act as conduits for federal dollars and as guarantors that such funds would be properly expended, but also setting the stage for evolving, fluctuating federalist relationships.

A further stage of federalism was reached with the Social Security Act of 1935, which authorized support for dependent children, the aged, and the blind, as well as for maternal and child health services, child welfare services, vocational rehabilitation, and public health services. This legislation was the "greatest impetus to a permanent state structure with primary responsibility for social welfare" (Vasey 1958, p. 379). By the end of the 1930s, state government had entered the administration of social programs generally and the administration of categorical efforts specifically. For its part, the federal government, in an effort to consolidate various human services, created the Federal Security Agency (1939), which housed the Social Security Board, the National Youth Administration, the Civilian Conservation Corps, the Public Health Service, the Office of Education, and the U.S. Employment Service. The intergovernmental partnership that foretold an increasingly national agenda in human services was firmly established (Axinn and Levin 1975), though as Gerry (in press) points out, that agenda was subject to change. Indeed, as we shall see later, the initiatives of the 1960s signaled a transformation in the federal role from one of universal protection via social insurance to one of social welfare and redistribution of wealth.

Although World War II clearly diverted attention to global issues, new domestic needs emerged. Women drawn into the domestic labor pool needed child care for their children, and the government provided it. During the war, women increasingly became heads of families, further temporarily broadening the rationale for social investments. Yet after the war, legitimated by the return of women to the home, public supports, such as for child care, diminished and a reversion to a loose patchwork of services—both in and out of government—occurred. Charitable organizations, including community chests and the United Way, ardently tried during this period to provide a semblance of order, with limited success owing in part to a persistently fluctuating federal role.

Though the federal role in human services had expanded considerably during the 1930s and 1940s, debates about how to execute such a role continued through the 1950s. For example, politicians and scholars considered alternative administrative structures. In 1950 the Hoover Commission recommended the creation of a cabinet-level department of social welfare, and in 1953 Dwight D. Eisenhower followed up by renaming the Federal Security Agency the Department of Health, Education and Welfare. States followed suit, with many undertaking reorganizations and forming "superagencies."

Still unsettled, federalist issues were addressed and readdressed during this period. Eisenhower told the National Governors Conference that he was running on a platform of states' rights. "I am here because of my indestructible conviction that unless we preserve, in this country, in the place of the State government, its traditional place—with the power, authority, the responsibilities and the revenue necessary to discharge those responsibilities—then we are not going to have an America as we have known it; we will have some other form of government" (Eisenhower 1953, p. 536). To ensure that such issues would receive ongoing attention, Congress established the Advisory Committee on Intergovernmental Relations in 1959. Congress need not have been too worried; federalist issues continued to command much attention in their own right in the coming decades.

Despite social scientists' intellectual infatuations with intergovernmental relations, in practice federal and state governments went to work independently each Monday. To be sure, there were exceptions— notably those efforts that had emerged during the New Deal to disperse responsibility for social issues—but the prevailing norm that framed governmental enterprise through the 1950s focused on the states as primarily sovereign entities. The typical federal assistance program did not involve a clearly enunciated national purpose. The federal government sought to promote efficiency and economy, but did not address substance. Programs were launched as a means of helping state or local governments accomplish their objectives. Typically, funds were distributed across the states according to a formula within broad statutory guidelines. When states developed plans that needed federal review, they were rarely rejected. Dubbed "dual" federalism or "layer cake" federalism where responsibilities were neatly divided (Zimmerman, 1983, p. 3)—and later, as governmental roles increased, "cooperative" federalism—federal and state governments were seen essentially as separate sovereignties with clearly delineated, independent spheres of activity.

One consequence of this federalist pattern was the significant discordance that arose between the federal government's expectations of the states (such as monitoring and enforcement) and the capacity of states to execute these roles. Compounding the problem, states varied tremendously in how much power they in turn accorded to localities. Analytically and practically, Dual Federalism fueled variation among the states and delimited federal authority over programs.

The Civil Rights Movement, the New Social Agenda, and the New Role of Government

A central influence on the human services structure after World War II was the civil rights movement. Gaining momentum annually, by the mid-1950s it had established legal protections (*Brown v. Board of Education of Topeka*) and mobilized support for an action agenda that focused on the plight of minorities and the poor. In this atmosphere of a new social consciousness, and encouraged by civil rights activists and social scientists who were eager to foster equity and promote human development, advocates for the disadvantaged espoused a variety of interventions. Moreover, unlike any previous time in American history, minorities established a collective voice and called for sweeping social changes.

Sundquist (1969) points out that as social problems develop, public attitudes pass through three phases. First, the problem is seen as local, outside the federal purview. Second, as understanding of the problem deepens, and as it becomes clear that states and localities cannot marshal the forces or resources to address it successfully, a federal response emerges to cope with what is still seen as a local or state problem. In the third phase, the focus shifts: the problem is recognized as a national issue, one that requires a national solution. Where civil rights were concerned, the country moved into the third phase with gusto. Few questioned whether the unrest in Watts or Newark or Detroit was a local problem. The civil rights movement and the inequities that provoked it were clearly a national issue calling for federal action.

Such acknowledgment may have been born either of moral obligation or of the hard reality that states could no longer function as isolated entities. The early 1960s witnessed the blossoming of a new era in interstate and federal-state relationships knitted together by advanced systems of communication and transportation and a unified national economy. Fervent discussions of state prerogatives were replaced by a coordinated federalism, one where national objectives were clear and policies defined, with the states acting as the conduits through which a national agenda was achieved.

In statute after statute, Congress during the 1960s affirmed this revamped federalist stance. President Lyndon B. Johnson, in elucidating his vision of a "Great Society," fortified this approach. The Great Society, by definition, was a unitary society made great by enmeshed commitments and strategies that would allow no state or community to inveigle itself out of just social commitments. Sustained by national resolve, the legislative and executive branches of government set forth an ambitious social agenda that had remarkable consequences for human services. With one foot in the door via the Social Security Act, the federal government plunged into the human services full force. Legislation burgeoned: the Manpower Development and Training Act and the Social Security Amendments of 1962; the Community Mental Health Act (1963); the Economic Opportunity Act and food stamp legislation (1964); Title XIII (Medicare) and Title XIX (Medicaid), the Elementary and Secondary Education Act, and Head Start legislation (1965); and

Social Security Amendments creating the Work Incentives (WIN) Program (1967); and the list goes on. Between 1962 and 1966 the number of federal categorical grant programs increased from 160 to 349, and by 1971 there were 500, totaling close to $30 billion for human service programs (Banfield 1971).

However promising these elements of "creative federalism"—as it was called—were, they raised serious structural and operational challenges. As the federalist structure was being transformed in the rush of legislation, little attention was paid to federal-state-local relations; the focus was on substance, not structure. There was no master plan. Sundquist quotes a government official of the time: "We have no organizational philosophy, only a program philosophy" (1969, p. 13). For example, the administrative structure of AFDC, the food stamp program, and Title I of the Elementary and Secondary Education Act operated on a state-to-local basis, while Head Start was federal-to-local and Social Security federal-to-state. In the absence of an overriding plan, each piece of legislation reflected the substantive intent of its particular framers. Some statutes invoked modes associated with Dual Federalism, others with Cooperative Federalism; some statutes called for formula grants, others for project grants; some lodged efforts in specified types of agencies, others called for the establishment of new agencies.

Although notably varied, most of these initiatives shared several structural properties. First, in addition to vastly expanding the role for the public sector, these efforts engaged the private sector more meaningfully than had previously been the case (Agranoff 1986). In so doing, they set the ideological stage for public-private partnerships.

Second, embroiled in efforts to achieve social equity, this generation of programs began to reshape the roles of clients and providers. Unlike those of past eras, many of these efforts hinged on the participation of the client in the planning of services (White and Gates 1974). Empowerment, client involvement, and family participation were regarded as the sine qua non of effective service delivery. The professional, once the paragon of knowledge, began to be viewed as one partner in the service delivery equation. Simultaneously, greater emphasis was placed on self-help and mutual aid, a relief to conservatives who saw such strategies as effective means of containing escalating social service costs.

Third, this array of federal initiatives were all created from special-purpose rather than general-purpose legislation and were categorically funded. Categorical grants identify problems and set priorities on a national basis and allocate resources on a targeted basis. Moreover, the funds generally carry with them restrictions on the administering agencies, eligible jurisdictions and participants, the programs' use of the money, and matching, planning, accountability, and personnel requirements. Categoricals, almost by definition, are restricted and difficult to coordinate.

And so out of the bevy of good intentions, chaos prevailed. So many local private, quasi-private, and public organizations received federal grants for various kinds of services that local mayors and even governors—recipients of the funds—were complaining by the mid-1960s. They could not keep track of the amount, locations, and services offered by the programs (Gilbert and Specht 1977). Such criticism, fortified by uncertain outcomes of many of the programs, diminished public support. Of even greater concern to government officials were efforts to create coordinating agencies outside of government in the form of Community Action Agencies. The rationale offered for lodging these agencies outside of government was multifold. First, it was felt that they needed to be community-driven and especially responsive to the low-income populations they served. The strategy implicitly condemned the capacity of conventional bureaucracies to meet the needs of the poor or to administer collaborative programs. Rather than hitch a rising star to the perceived dead weight of staid bureaucracies, new agencies, it was thought, would be more effective.

Formed in 1964 as the prime instrument of Johnson's War on Poverty, Community Action Agencies (CAA) were established to foster local-level coordination. "Community action was repeatedly described as a device that would draw federal, state, and local programs together and meld them into an integrated assault upon the problems of poverty"

The Historical Perspective

(Sundquist 1969, p. 35). The vision was that CAAs would have a planning capacity that would cut across community agencies and sectors, and that in mobilizing public and private community resources they would engage in various linkage strategies: case management, outreach and case finding, client advocacy, and collocation of activities. Using their flexible dollars, CAAs would fill programmatic gaps according to community need. Moreover, to fortify their coordinative role, CAAs were given authority to comment on projects of other local organizations, including those emanating from the departments of Housing and Urban Development (HUD), Health, Education and Welfare (HEW), and Labor.

Despite their clear charge and important supports, CAAs achieved only limited results in their coordination efforts (Kramer 1969). In part, this could have been anticipated. The disengagement of the poverty agencies from city halls did little to engender support or to hasten intraprogram or intersector coordination. Often CAAs found themselves competing with an elaborate network of planning vehicles or other organizational entities that were authorized to assume a planning function, including chambers of commerce, housing agencies, boards of education, churches, and the United Way. Called "decision organizations" by Warren (1967), these entities carried considerable weight in communities and typically predated CAAs, many of whom were still fledgling organizations ill-equipped to compete with established and well-recognized planning entities. In addition, CAAs were often considered ideological and partisan. Many Republicans contended that the bill establishing CAAs, an outgrowth of Democratic goals, was stampeded through Congress with insufficient debate. Such sentiments were echoed at the local level, where prominent Republicans in key community positions did little to support CAAs. Moreover, CAAs were often regarded as misconceived and mismanaged, agents of advocacy and confrontation. Finally, in some communities the programs were criticized because they were thought to replicate existing efforts. Particularly in the cases of employment services and Head Start, CAAs were charged with service duplication or the usurpation of services previously thought destined to reside within welfare and education, respectively. Rather than exemplars of coordination, CAAs were often—though not necessarily accurately—criticized for being demagogues of duplication.

Experiencing "Creative" Federalism

Early on, President Johnson became aware of the difficulties associated with CAAs. In his budget message of January 1966 he called for strengthening CAAs and their coordinative role in communities (Johnson 1966). Echoing the concern, Senator Edmund Muskie, then chairman of the Senate Subcommittee on Intergovernmental Relations, presented a detailed analysis of the coordination problems at all levels of government and called for a series of remedial measures, including new coordinating mechanisms. At the national level, he proposed a national intergovernmental affairs council, paralleling the National Security Council. At the departmental level, he called for an undersecretary with full-time responsibility for coordinating programs on departmental, interdepartmental, and intergovernmental bases. At the regional level, his committee endorsed the establishment of federal regional coordinators. And at the local level, he called for a federal coordinator in every city.

A hearing held by the subcommittee affirmed the seriousness of the problem, as members of the president's cabinet testified to the lack of coordination in government. It was noted that "[c]oordination among Federal agencies leaves much to be desired. Communication between the various levels of government—federal, state and local—is casual and ineffective. State and local government is in most areas seriously inadequate" (Hearings before the Subcommittee 1966).

Responses to the pleas for coordination took many forms. Electing to focus on systems of negotiation among equals rather than the imposition of hierarchical authority, the federal government designated functional coordinators by field (the secretary of housing and urban development was made responsible for coordinating urban development, the secretary of agriculture for rural development, and so on). Coordinators were assigned and reassigned so frequently that one of the group referred to the process irreverently as the "coordinator of the month club" (Sundquist 1969, p. 20). The coordinators were to assist and advise the president and were to establish cross-cabinet interdepartmental committees to coordinate efforts. The director of the Office of Economic Opportunity (OEO) became the point person, with particular responsibility for coordinating the War on Poverty; Vice President Hubert H. Humphrey was designated as the contact person with mayors. Though appearing organized, the system—characterized by its own lack of specificity and duplication of efforts—had severe limitations; its loose and somewhat redundant structure predicted its outcome: only modest success.

Augmenting this federal structure, links were made to communities predicated on the understanding that coordination gaps at the federal level directly curtailed the ability of local and state agencies to coordinate. However correct the conception, there was another problem: the local communities did not always have the capacity to support coordinative efforts. Many federal agencies, therefore, developed community mobilization plans, and dozens of Washington-initiated but locally implemented planning entities were established, each reflecting a unique constituency and mission. These efforts added responsibilities to already burdened local administrators, so that rather than eradicating the fragmentation generated in Washington, they helped perpetuate it.

Disjointed as these efforts were, they also helped to clarify the complex coordination issues and lay the groundwork for new alternatives. Jordan (1971) observes that they taught what not to do. By revisiting the collective and largely negative lessons of the early CAAs regarding coordination, and the rudimentary attempts at federally initiated coordination, policymakers—it was hoped—could devise a more promising strategy.

Not precisely derivative of these efforts but reflecting a growing body of practical knowledge, the Model Cities initiative was launched by President Johnson in 1967, barely a year after his vociferous commitments to the War on Poverty and to CAAs. Model Cities was the linchpin of an effort that, though called "new," sounded remarkably similar to

CAAs. Emanating from a task force on urban problems chaired by Robert Wood, then of the Massachusetts Institute of Technology, the Model Cities concept was designed to redress concerns regarding the displacement of the poor that had resulted from HUD's misguided efforts. Its aim was to address the physical and social environments of urban poverty, and hence it was a natural link to the already established social agenda. It seemed to offer brighter prospects of more comprehensive and effective coordination. The CAAs, then quite young, did not seem comprehensive enough as many agencies had begun to focus on direct service delivery, advocacy, and confrontation as means to achieve those ends. Rejecting such tactics, Wood and his colleagues offered an alternative approach, one that put coordinated, comprehensive planning before action.

After participating in a preliminary review, 63 successful communities were given a year to plan their Model Cities efforts with federal dollars. Shortly thereafter, an additional 12 programs were supported. Ultimately, 150 cities participated in the planning, having at their disposal almost as much money as would be expended by all the CAAs in the nation. Early evaluations looked promising; Sundquist (1969) indicates that by the end of the 1968 planning year, the communities had accomplished a "remarkable achievement in coordination" (p. 102). Three factors seemed to contribute to this success. First, the Model Cities structure needed to be accountable to community residents *and* to provide for the meaningful participation of city hall and structured government. Second, the demonstration agencies needed not to operate programs directly but to concentrate on their roles as coordinators, collaborators, and planners. Finally, the organization had to be representative of the total neighborhood, and not be reduced to a small clique empowered to speak for all.

Looking back, Gilbert and Specht (1977) note instructive findings relevant to subsequent coordination and service integration. They found that coordination efforts in the Model Cities initiative tended to be most successful in medium-sized communities (population of

100,000–140,000), with small cities often suffering because of the lack of professional expertise. The analysis also indicated a positive correlation between a city's past and present success in coordination. The support and leadership of the chief executive were important predictors of success, as was the ability to engage other public and private sector agencies in the effort. Thus, the Model Cities apparatus provided a promising, albeit not the sole or perfect, mechanism for collaboration and service integration.

At the time these efforts were being launched, however, skepticism regarding the domestic agenda was clouded by an unpopular foreign war and an increasingly unpopular president. Creative Federalism was tainted—regarded as a reflection of social conditions so blighted that only intensive intervention from federal, state, and local governments could begin to ameliorate escalating problems. The programs—though insufficient time had elapsed to render suitable evaluation—were publicly perceived to be mired in confusion. Centralization, under whatever guise, led to the proliferation of programs that were deemed to have no clear goals, no clear target audience, and ineffective methods of accountability. Though some flexibility of implementation was necessary to accommodate broad goals, few could ignore the mounting red tape, the organizational inefficiency, and a decided sense that the system was out of control. Governors, mayors, and county executives did not know who was making the decisions, but it was clear that they were not. Ink (1973) notes that one of the most serious drawbacks to the Creative Federalism of the Johnson era was that the system "increasingly undercut state and local leadership" (p. 30). Like pawns without authority, they were victims of the overcommitment and underfunding that began to take place as resources were diverted to the war effort. The credibility of the federal government plummeted, as those Johnson sought most desperately to help—the poor—suffered from broken hopes and false starts. Following the death of Martin Luther King, Jr., America's ghettos went up in flames, taking with them the dreams of a nation at odds with itself.

The New Federalism

Against this backdrop, Richard M. Nixon assumed the presidency in 1969. The New Federalism, his approach to distributing authority across levels of government, contrasted sharply with Johnson's Creative Federalism, but it skillfully built on the lessons of the past. The Nixon administration recognized that Johnson's brand of federalism, for all its ills, had addressed the interaction of the three levels of government. Though underscoring a commitment to the importance of all three levels, Nixon's New Federalism clearly indicated that they could not expect to have equal control over all tasks of government, and preferred that states and localities have the lion's share. Keeping government close to the people and strengthening the role of elected officials at the state and local levels framed Nixon's reorganization strategies. Through the establishment of standard federal regions, program decentralization, simplification of federal grant processes, and revenue sharing, the Nixon agenda began to take hold.

Two important characteristics of the New Federalism were its emphasis on general purpose governments and its concern with service integration, both reactions to the excesses of the Johnson era. General purpose governments, defined as the subfederal levels of government, include states, counties, towns, and municipalities. Often, they are equated with the individual executives who are responsible for these entities (such as governors and mayors). Gardner (1976) suggests that there are two types of executives in general purpose governments: (1) political executives who assume office as a result of the political process, via election or direct appointment as senior managing official of government; and (2) general executives who have constitutional authority ranging across branches of government and who are not running a circumscribed agency of government. The more expansive Gardner definition includes, along with governors and mayors, city managers, county executives, and planning and budget officials.

The New Federalism favored these generalists over specialists and favored general purpose governments over functional agencies that had been the primary recipients of categorical funding. Nathan (1975),

The Historical Perspective

an architect of the New Federalism, writes: "The federal government should stay out of the thicket of state-local government structure, being neutral among different types and levels of general purpose units of local governments" (p. 126).

The term *service integration* came into popular usage at this time, although the construct was hardly new. It was, however, taking on new shades of meaning and a new aura. Gardner (1976) notes that the original hopes for a "coordinative function to be played by local community agencies fell prey within two years to much more intensive issues of advocacy and survival" (p. 6). He goes on to say that service integration of the New Federalism represented a substantially different position than that of the past because its "unmanageability" was at stake.

Both these constructs—general purpose governments and service integration—were seen as correctives to Great Society ills. General purpose governments attempted to stave off the by-passing of local governments characteristic of community action. Service integration attempted to correct categorical excesses by channeling resources to meet the needs of the whole person, reflecting developmental theories that were gaining currency at the time.

Whatever their heritage, general purpose government and service integration were welded into an ideologically integrated construct that defined, perhaps more clearly than ever before, the role of a federal agency. A statement by the secretary of HEW, Casper Weinberger, proclaimed the commitment of that department to help chief executives and local general purpose governments improve their capacities to plan and manage human service programs (U.S. Department of Health, Education and Welfare 1975a, cited in Gardner 1976). Four components of capacity building were specified: (1) departmental policy reforms; (2) development and dissemination of information and technology; (3) better technical assistance; and (4) demonstration grants. Weinberger's statement appears to have derived from the experience of the department because many of the activities in the preceding years from 1969 to 1975 conformed to these components.

The statement must, however, be approached with caution. First, it suggests that much of the principal activity of the era was at the federal level. This is not accurate: some of the most effective service integration efforts were not only lodged at the local and state level but funded by state and local resources. Gardner (1976) cites Wisconsin as an example, and Lynn (1980) notes that in Georgia and Washington State gubernatorial leadership was noteworthy, while in Arizona and Florida state legislatures provided much impetus for service integration.

Second, it assumes that much of the impetus occurred in at HEW. Though HEW did take a critical lead on the service integration agenda, efforts were under way in other departments, including Labor and HUD. Furthermore, describing the "fourth face of federalism," Kettl (1984) notes that it was in "manpower and community development programs, mainly for cities, that the 'new' federalism bore fruit" (p. 290). Kettl is referring to the Comprehensive Employment and Training Act of 1973 and the Community Development Block Grants of 1974, both of which not only left major planning to the localities but also furthered the engagement of nongovernmental groups in human services through contracting mechanisms. In this sense, service integration (and other coordination efforts) created a fourth face of federalism, one that included significant engagement from nongovernmental agencies. So important are these to the human services generally and to service integration in particular that Agranoff (1986) notes that "to speak of intergovernmental relations in contemporary human services is to include nongovernmental actors tied to the public sector" (p. 24).

Finally, though constructs like general purpose government and service integration seem tidy, they are no more easily implemented than their predecessors. Indeed, passing the responsibility for dividing up resources to the state and local levels proved equally complex. Because of their inherently redistributive nature—wherein resources are allocated to the poorest populations—distributing funds among human service programs is inherently difficult for elected officials. Such difficulty is accelerated by the growth in citizen participation of the 1960s, wherein citizens feel obligated to express their ideas, however contentious. Many elected officials, finding the heat of such debate too hot, withdrew from the distribution of human service dollars. In reality, then, the New Federalism was an era of tension characterized by political disincentives as well as mixed governmental and managerial incentives.

Service Integration from the 1970s to the Present

The early 1970s were a vibrant time for service integration, with many initiatives—described in detail in the following chapters—taking root. Some were initiated by HEW, and some by other federal agencies. Some were established to improve direct client services, whereas others focused on broader systemic or policy reform. The early 1970s provided some of our most thorough research initiatives and some of the most comprehensive service integration policy initiatives to date. As such, the era set the stage for all future work in the field.

Paradoxically, perhaps the most important lesson was that however robust and widespread, these efforts were contextually bound and operationally comparatively short-lived. Indeed, federal initiative waned during the late 1970s, as individuals turned attention toward reversing program expansion.

The Carter years were marked by a lull in domestic policy. Though President Jimmy Carter actually introduced an enormous number of bills for congressional action, including welfare reform, there is little evidence that his presidency established priorities to guide Congress or that the White House made any concerted effort to lobby for the passage of bills. Indeed, "very little was accomplished through Congressional action" (Abernathy 1984, p. 122), save the establishment of a separate Department of Education in July 1979 and the formation of the Department of Health and Human Services (HHS)—changes that had more of a "symbolic than structural interest for the President" (Hill 1984, p. 24).

With the election of Ronald Reagan as president came a strong commitment to devolution of authority to the states and a desire to reduce human service expenditures. In the early 1980s, block grants became the norm, ostensibly as a primary vehicle to integrate services. In effect, the block grant apparatus, because it was accompanied by significant fiscal cuts, did the opposite. Providers scrambled for limited dollars, competing with one another at every turn. Rather than furnishing strategies that would overcome the problem of service fragmentation, Reagan's federalism exacerbated the need for collaboration and integration while militating against its accomplishment.

With the social service system becoming less cohesive and social problems far more complex, the mid- to late 1980s saw the evolution of numerous grass-roots responses to overcome the polemics of fragmentation. State and local governments and private institutions often intervened at the behest of service providers who could no longer deal with the systemic pain they were experiencing. The locus for invention moved from the federal to the state and local level, and from the federal pocketbook to the portfolios of foundations. This era of "unplanned" variation supplied some rich examples of strategies and some novel conceptual approaches that reemphasized the role of the provider at the local level and the role of the client. Capturing the intent of the 1960s to empower those who needed services, many of the service integration efforts of the 1980s and 1990s have had a sharp focus on the service- or client-based approach to integration. Of those that concentrate on broader systemic reform, the client-first, bottom-up emphasis seems to prevail.

That so many diverse approaches to service integration began to emerge simultaneously caused the federal government, long interested in the issue, to reconsider its role. As the 1990s dawned, new initiatives were being considered within and among federal agencies. Special efforts accompanied by funding were launched to provide technical support to those implementing service integration efforts, and a national clearinghouse, part of the National Center for Service Integration, was formed to address conceptual and practical challenges in the field.

Deep roots in American history, going back to colonial times, have kept service integration alive through droughts of attention from society and government. It remains a strategy of importance as the problems of delivering a vast array of human services become more and more complex. No longer waiting for federal impetus, workers in human services are moving forward on their own. It is to the lessons that we can garner from them and from their predecessors that we now turn.

2

Federal Approaches: Research and Demonstration

Federal work on service integration followed two primary strategies in the early to mid-1970s: a research and demonstration strategy and a legislative strategy. To set the stage for a detailed discussion of research and demonstration in this chapter and legislation in the next, let us begin by elucidating the context in which these strategies arose.

The Context for Research and Legislative Action

A major impetus for engagement in the service integration agenda emanated from efforts to find programmatic expression for the New Federalism. Though not a major participant in the War on Poverty until later, the Department of Health, Education and Welfare was to become quite a pioneer in the service integration efforts. Yessian (1991) suggests that there were two precipitating factors for HEW's interest, or more specifically the interest of its secretary, Elliot Richardson. First, there was the desire to separate income maintenance and social services, presumably to give greater visibility to social services and remove it from the welfare quagmire. Second, there was the secretary's own interest in service integration and his willingness to use the power of his office to call attention to issues of human services organization, decisions that are, "at bottom, decisions about human services policy" (Lynn 1980, p. 7). In a now famous speech, Richardson lamented the burgeoning number of categorical programs, the burdens that such complexities impose on families, and the impediment to effectiveness and efficiency that such fragmentation poses. In referring to the "hardening of the categories," the secretary went on record as supporting reform with service integration as its centerpiece.

Richardson was quite correct in his perception of the situation. In the years between 1961 and the early 1970s the number of HEW programs tripled to exceed 300. According to an internal undated and unsigned document, 54 of the programs overlapped each other and 36 overlapped programs in other departments in significant ways. Federal rules and regulations for the HEW programs were "highly prescriptive, restrictive, duplicative and conflicting," with more than 1,200 pages in the Federal Register devoted to program administration; and each of these pages, in turn, required an average of ten additional pages of interpretive guidelines. Not limited to the federal government, such chaos prevailed at the state level as well. Individual states at this time averaged between 80 and 100 separate social service administrations, and the average community had between 400 and 500 human service providers.

Though these conditions were sufficient in themselves, other rationales added impetus to the press for service integration and the secretary's commitment to it. Material from the heretofore confidential Dolson files is quite revealing. In correspondence dated April 6, 1971, from Jonathan Moore, it appears that the secretary was also interested in two further goals: "(1) to enable major on-going service programs

(VR [vocational rehabilitation], welfare, Head Start Services . . .) to expand their programs at the delivery level in order to be able to provide each others' services where appropriate and acceptable, and (2) be able to fund project grants applications for multi-service efforts beyond legislative categorical constraints." To accomplish this, several strategies were proposed:

> (a) amend the enabling legislation for each program so that a portion (all?) of the regular appropriation can be used by the Federal Administrator for additional purposes at the delivery level; (b) propose one piece of enabling legislation which creates a specific kind of rider to a regular state plan or project application which seeks support for broadening services at the delivery point and which, if the secretary approves, permits the use of funds appropriated for another categorical program; or (c) create a new pot of money for funding new services added on to categorical programs at the delivery level. (M. Linsky, qtd. Moore 1971, p. 3)

It was suggested that legislative action be taken, building on a research and demonstration effort "which ELR [Richardson] feels we are ready for." However, despite overall enthusiasm, such initiatives included certain drawbacks. It was unclear how regional planning and administration could be taken into account unless funds were made available for regional or local umbrella planning agents. Further, little incentive seemed to exist for such service integration at the local level, in part because "unrelated showcases" of the secretary put little pressure on locals to integrate health and welfare programs. (It should be noted that such attempts were made in the withdrawn Title XX legislation.) Finally, according to Moore, some related legislative action was being considered: notably, a feeder bill to be tacked on to the Brademas-Dellenbach bill.

To address these concerns, the secretary had established several governmental task forces to try to meet "head-on the problems created within HEW's vast network of programs." The Research and Development Task Force was under the auspices of the Office of the Secretary/Assistant Secretary for Planning and Evaluation; the Task Force on

Service Integration Barriers and Constraints was under the auspices of the Office of the Secretary/Assistant Secretary of Community Development; and a third task force, for the development of legislation, was under the auspices of the Office of the Secretary/Assistant Secretary of Legislation (Solarz 1973). Moreover, the impetus for such efforts was reinforced by interest at the Office of Management and Budget (OMB) to streamline grant programs and to improve intra- and interdepartmental coordination. The Department of Health, Education and Welfare had established its own Federal Assistance Streamlining Task Force (FAST) to expedite grants, devolve authority to the regions and field offices, and integrate services.

Despite all this activity, in the spring of 1972 there was grave concern that service integration was still in an embryonic stage. Recognizing the paucity of knowledge both within and outside HEW, the HEW task forces affirmed that the federal government could assist states and local governments to reform services delivery, but if they were to do so effectively such work needed to be guided by more knowledge. The task forces concurred that "there was a lack of precise knowledge as to the nature of the problem" (Kurzman n.d., p. 4). Moreover, internal analysis concluded that a major emphasis should be "toward the development, testing and utilization of specific models for service integration within the legislative and administrative bounds obtaining" (Solarz 1973, p. 845). It was in this context that legislative and research-and-demonstration initiatives were launched. The intention of using research results to inform legislation was an explicit strategy that gave birth to and legitimated a growing interest in the series of research and demonstration efforts that were to follow.

Services Integration Targets of Opportunity Projects

Recognizing the paucity of real understanding about service integration, the federal government undertook several major research and demonstration initiatives. By 1972, these were often referred to as the Allied Services Act pre-test projects. In particular, the Services Integration

Targets of Opportunity (SITO) projects were designed to be an advance guard of the legislation and to provide a source of data on its prospective utility.

Initiated by HEW in June 1972, the SITO projects sought information about methods of integrating services, constraints on service integration, and the effects of service integration on clients and service delivery systems. The term *targets of opportunity*—borrowed by Sidney Gardner (personal communication, November 1992) from the military, where it connoted sudden opportunities for attack, for which one should be prepared to react instantly—was adopted to reflect the intent of the projects to determine the locus (target) where feasible administrative intervention could modify practice. "SITO was not a social experiment designed by central staff" (Fishman and Dolson n.d., p. 5) nor was it an HEW attempt to impose a single approach to service integration. Rather, it encouraged grantees to formulate their own procedures to assess and address problems. Indeed, SITO projects were selected with the objective of providing the broadest possible base for demonstration of various service integration techniques. Diversity not only characterized the projects' internal approaches and overall goals, but was also manifest in the nature, duration, and recipients of funding. In total, 45 SITO projects were funded at a cost of about $12 million, with 10 being carried out by consulting firms or public interest groups. The other 35, many of which were funded for three years, were comprehensive service delivery efforts carried out by state or local governments or private agencies.

The SITO projects were launched with several service integration goals in mind: to enhance outcomes for special target groups; to create integrated service entities such as community schools or community mental health centers; to provide incentives for service area consolidation; to enhance the involvement of volunteer agencies; and to broaden the role of general purpose government in coordinating services for clients. Though launched with these multiple goals in mind, the SITO projects tended to neglect the goal related to client outcome and focus on process lessons. In fact, a Rand analysis concluded that the "absence of data on client outcomes *across most projects* severely limits any type of evaluation and limits what can be said about service integration. In particular, one cannot test the central assumption that service integration is either necessary or valuable" (Lucas 1975, p. 4). (This conclusion led Rand to recommend an alternate strategy—a research census—to develop findings in SITO and non-SITO projects [Lucas, Heald, and Vogel 1975].) Equally ardent, Soler and Shauffer (1990) attacked the fundamental design of SITO, noting that it failed because its architects were insensitive to the political and social realities of the communities it intended to serve.

The Rand study and others acknowledged, however, that many of the projects, despite their diversity and the lack of generalizability of results, did contribute to the knowledge of service delivery strategies. A predominant effect of SITO has been the creation of new mechanisms, "usually at the community or sub-state level that can be considered important ingredients of systems: client pathways, common intake forms, service taxonomies, case managers, information systems, research and planning capability, funding mechanisms, internal performance measures, service contracts, specification and audit procedures, governance bodies, single-point management functions, and many others" (Mittenthal 1975, p. 81).

Results of the SITO efforts are far from conclusive, with little hard data affirming alterations in nontechnical approaches or in cost-effectiveness. For example, data do not verify any increase in accessibility and availability of services. To some it became clear that such coordinative efforts were expensive in terms of human and fiscal resources, leading one researcher to conclude that such efforts are unlikely to cut costs (Fishman and Dolson n.d., p. 8). But given the lack of normative information on what an ideal system is or what it costs, such gaps in the knowledge generated were not unexpected.

On the positive side, SITO did help clarify the processes associated with service integration. For example, we learned that most of the SITO projects failed to distinguish between the development and the implementation of integration strategies, a fact that often led to imprecise accountability and inflated expectations. The analyses affirmed the importance of the contextual setting (such as demography and history) and the need to achieve a balance between public- and private-sector engagement. Perhaps most important, SITO data reaffirmed the "formidable constraints—political, institutional, legislative, administrative, financial, etc. to initiating and executing human service development programs" (Mittenthal 1975, p. 83).

Though helpful to practitioners and planners, the SITO work left a huge policy void in its wake. Despite its impetus as a "legislative pretest," it failed to answer some of the fundamental issues, outlined by Lynn and Sprague (1972), that led to its initiation: the optimal size of service delivery areas, the transferability of experience from one size service area to another, effective methodologies for performing needs assessments and analyses, methodologies for discerning client impact and the measures to do so, and strategies regarding confidentiality. Such findings, however important, would need to wait for a further iteration of service integration research.

The Partnership Grants Program

As noted earlier, one of the primary commitments of HEW was to help chief executives and local general purpose governments to improve their capacities to plan and manage human service programs. To that end, the Partnership Grants Program (PGP) was launched in fiscal year 1974.

Recognizing that excessive fragmentation existed at all levels of government, that the nation was taking piecemeal approaches to complex issues, and that there was a lack of accountability for the performance of programs on the part of elected officials, the PGP provided seed money to states, substate regions, cities, counties, and city/county areas to supplement ongoing system reform efforts. Objectives ranged from the tactical, such as assessing human service needs, to the strategic, including efforts to define the roles of general purpose government in human service delivery. Such a variety of objectives, however, made evaluating the PGP difficult. Moreover, because service integration was catching on in communities, it was hard to isolate the impact of the PGP from other efforts in the community or state.

Though the 84 PGP projects cost an estimated $9.1 million, its lessons are limited. Resembling the SITO results in that the most important lessons were process-oriented, the PGP effort added additional contextual information to the repertoire of knowledge. For example, it affirmed that the political environment in a jurisdiction exercises a major influence on the type of human service reform agenda that can be pursued and that the role of the chief can determine project outcome; it also rekindled the need to define and understand barriers to integration. Sadly, however, the PGP data were not sufficiently robust or definitive to be generalizable.

Comprehensive Human Services Planning and Delivery System Projects

The experience with SITO and the PGP, as well as the growing number of responsibilities devolving to the states and localities, stimulated a new effort aimed primarily at problems associated with local planning and management. Concern was mounting that despite all the efforts to integrate services, responsibility at the local level had so dramatically proliferated that the municipalities were compared to developing nations. Bereft of capacity to handle the massive infusion of authority, these "developing communities" needed assistance. Moreover, there was concern that with the amalgamation of state agencies—a trend well under way, with 26 states having some form of comprehensive agency—greater accountability would be required and that states would, in turn, heap additional burdens of accountability on local communities.

Not conceived as a panacea, the Comprehensive Human Services Planning and Delivery System (CHSPDS) projects, launched in 1975, were explicitly designed to yield useful data. The research and demonstration objectives were quite specific:

(1) to develop and field test models for local level comprehensive planning and management of social services;

(2) to develop techniques and methods for generating accurate data bases—need assessment, resources inventorying, system monitoring, and client monitoring;

(3) to develop and demonstrate planning and management control technologies with direct applicability to comprehensive social services planning by local general purpose government;

(4) to evaluate the impact of comprehensive human services planning and delivery on the effectiveness and efficiency of the delivery systems. (Comprehensive Human Services Planning and Delivery n.d., p. 1)

Planners did not expect to generalize their results to other locales; rather, they were interested in probing a limited number of hypotheses in a few sites that had the potential to render helpful insights. To affirm its overall hypothesis that the "comprehensive planning of services at the local and state level will significantly improve the impact, responsiveness and efficiency of the service delivery system" (p. 14), sub-hypotheses to be tested at all sites were generated and ten management elements were required to be in place at the end of two years: (1) a taxonomy of service and problems, (2) an effects audit system, (3) a cost accounting system, (4) a social problem analysis, (5) a community resources inventory, (6) a management information system, (7) a client tracking system, (8) a case management system, (9) an information and referral system, and (10) community objectives.

Ultimately, five sites (Brockton and Taunton, Mass.; Louisville/Jefferson County, Ky.; Portsmouth, Va.; and Suffolk County, N.Y.), representing diverse organizational structures and community settings, were selected for the project. Specification of goals, coupled with judicious selection of sites, yielded some promising findings. One project was so successful that it was replicated in six other geopolitical areas of the state (Fishman and Dolson n.d., p. 15). Near the end of the project, evaluators noted rich contributions of the work: effective use of management elements can shorten the waiting time for clients, ensure accountability and the adequacy of services, and result in more efficient use of resources.

The project ended, after several years, in an era of reorganization and fiscal constraint. Changes were made in staff and programs were transferred at the national level and, even more consequentially, fiscal cutbacks made full implementation in the third year impossible and prevented an independent third-party evaluation.

Services Integration Pilot Projects

Though occurring significantly later in history (1984), the Services Integration Pilot Projects (SIPP) marked the last in the line of general service integration efforts. Born of a different context, some of the SIPP goals sound remarkably familiar: to improve the management and delivery of human services and to promote the capacity of individuals and families to achieve or maintain self-sufficiency. Rather than articulating effective management as the sole goal, however, the SIPP made it quite clear that effective management is a means to achieve individual self-sufficiency.

The SIPP—a product of the Reagan era—was born from a desire to contain costs and to help reduce the federal deficit. In fact, the SIPP authorization is contained in Section 1136 of the Social Security Act, which was established as Section 2630 of the Deficit Reduction Act of 1984, P.L. 98–369. It was thought that such reductions could be accomplished by streamlining services and eliminating duplication and unnecessary waste. In addition, demands on the federal pocketbook could be reduced by increasing the number of individuals who were self-sufficient and lowering the number on welfare. Thus, embedded in the SIPP mission is a clear sense of system *and* individual accountability. Not unexpectedly, the SIPP calls for clearly evaluating client outcomes in addition to specifying that delivery systems "develop and demonstrate ways of improving the delivery of services to individuals and families who need them under the various human service programs, by eliminating programmatic fragmentation and thereby assuring that an applicant for services under one such program will be informed and have access to all of the services which may be available to him or his family under the other human service programs being carried out in the community" (CSR, 1986, p. 1).

Unlike in the past, when localities and private organizations were eligible to participate in such programs, primary eligibility was now limited to states, with awards going to five—Arizona, Florida, Maine, Oklahoma, and South Carolina. During the planning year, beginning May 1, 1985, states were to develop a scientifically sound strategy to evaluate system and client outcomes. Technical assistance was provided to grantees for developing the design, methodology, and measures to be used. Funding for the SIPP was authorized at a level of $8 million, but Congress appropriated no money in the first or second year. Support for the SIPP came in these years from discretionary funds in the Office of Human Development Services (HDS), a part of the Department of Health and Human Services. Lacking sufficient funding, HDS turned to other federal agencies for help, and three agencies contributed to the effort: the Labor Departments's Administration on Employment and Training; the Family Support Administration's Office of Family Assistance, and the Administration on Aging. This integration of funding, coupled with a required federal Interdepartmental Work Group, made the funding and administration of the SIPP an integrated effort in itself.

The projects constituted a variety of structures and plans to integrate an array of services, ranging from three services in Florida to all needs-based services in Arizona and South Carolina. Some projects, like in Maine and South Carolina, covered their entire territory, while others targeted cities or counties (Arizona, for example, selected Flagstaff). Each state (or substate unit) took a client-centered approach with the primary goal of using various service integration mechanisms to support a case management approach to service delivery.

Though comprehensive and conclusive outcome data on the SIPP are not available, a September 1989 evaluative report notes that "a key insight is that implementation and replication of pilot projects must have the support of those within the system as well as members of the community. A foundation of support from local and state policy makers, in-house power brokers, employees, case workers, clients and community leaders must be established" (State Reorganization Commission 1989, p. 53). More broadly, Fishman and Dolson (n.d.) note that the SIPP represents the pulling together and the testing of many of the delivery mechanisms that have evolved over the past years. Reflecting optimism, they suggest that the outcome orientation of the SIPP, and related efforts, bodes well for advancing the delivery of integrated services to the poor.

The tenacity with which recurrent efforts have pursued an evaluation-to-policy agenda is impressive. Were the evaluations sufficiently helpful to inform policy? Were they stepping stones to a more elaborated research agenda? Did they contribute to or complicate the policy agenda? To answer these questions, let us examine service integration policy initiatives of the 1970s and 1980s.

3

Federal Approaches: Legislation

Returning to the earliest of the research and demonstration efforts, we note that the Services Integration Targets of Opportunity projects were conceptualized and implemented to guide legislation, indicating both an early recognition of the lack of confidence that Congress would set its own agenda for integrating services, and a recognition that hard evidence was needed to build political support. Sadly, such thinking proved to be prescient. The shortcomings of service integration research and demonstration projects discussed in chapter 2 provide the prologue for examining the equally troubled history of service integration legislation that the research and development efforts were designed to support.

The Legislative Panorama

In the early 1970s, service integration was the focus of much legislative effort. Solarz (1973) noted eleven such legislative initiatives:

(1) The Intergovernmental Cooperation Act (ICA) as enacted in 1968 and as proposed for amendment in 1972.

(2) The Allied Services Act (ASA) of 1972, then undergoing reassessment before being reintroduced.

(3) Special Revenue Sharing as proposed in the areas of education, manpower, and community development.

(4) The Integrated Grants Administration (IGA) in OMB.

(5) Switching Station (Division of Consolidated Funding) in HEW.

(6) The Responsive Governments Act (RGA) proposed by HUD.

(7) Law Enforcement Assistance Planning (LEA) authorized under and administered by the Department of Justice.

(8) Comprehensive Areawide Manpower Planning Systems (CAMPS) administered by the Department of Labor.

(9) Comprehensive Health Planning (CHP)—a program in HEW authorized under the Partnership for Health Act of 1966.

(10) Areawide Aging Grants within HEW as authorized under the 1972 amendments to the Older Americans Act of 1968.

(11) Community Consolidated Child Care (4C) within HEW as administered by the Office of Child Development.

This critical trend toward integration suggested the breadth of concern regarding service integration that pervaded government. Clearly, service integration was not the hobbyhorse of one secretary or one department. Moreover, such commitment to change signaled that although rejecting the strategies of the Johnson era and Creative Federalism in favor of the New Federalism, policymakers had sufficient faith in the power of the government to do something about the problem. Elected officials as well as energetic bureaucrats were poised to act; they carried with them the confidence that they could make the system better.

But to do so meant a comprehensive strategy that would engage all levels of government, as well as private agencies and frontline, field-based providers. Reflecting the sentiment of the time, the secretary spoke with HEW employees in December 1971 on "Responsibility and Responsiveness":

> Cutting away red tape, grant packaging, and grant consolidation will, separately and in combination, make Federal support less hampering and more useful. They will help to bring about more comprehensive, less categorical service delivery systems. But the fragmentation of services is by no means a consequence solely of Federal policies and procedures, and cannot be overcome by Federal action alone.
>
> At the community level, the agencies devoted to helping people are too numerous, too limited in function, and too isolated from each other. Local agencies tend to be fully as jealous in protecting their own turf as any Federal entity. Professional disciplines do not lose their guildmindedness at the local level. . . .
>
> It is not enough, therefore, simply to improve the ability of each provider of services to perform its particular role. We must also promote communication among the various service providers, joint planning among them, coordinated program operations, and comprehensive systems dealing with the needs of people. (Richardson 1972)

The Feeder Bill of 1971

Recognizing the magnitude of the problem, officials within HEW considered various options for the amelioration of the situation. Alternatives included the research and demonstration strategy discussed above and various tag-ons to extant legislation. However, it seemed to HEW officials and to the deliberating task forces established by Secretary Richardson that these strategies were insufficient in scope or magnitude. Instead, early efforts turned toward crafting a piece of coordinative, though not omnibus, legislation that would be the basic mechanism for coordinating services delivery into which categorical bills would feed— hence the name "feeder bill."

From internal documents (Twiname 1971a), it is clear that HEW officials recognized the staying power of categorical grants and rejected the idea of an omnibus bill into which operational categoricals would be folded. Similarly, they realized that no new initiative should be predicated on the assumption of abolishment of other major service acts or should be unrelated to the existing service delivery system. On the other hand, the early framers wanted a sufficiently powerful act that "could be counted upon to lead toward some degree of reform of services" (Twiname 1971a, p. 1).

In addition, the new bill needed to permit flexibility for the governors and the secretary. Limitations on the secretary arising from his lack of legislative authority proved detrimental to accomplishing the service integration agenda. Governors needed to be released from onerous regulations so that they could reorganize state governments more effectively.

To balance these concerns in an effort that was administratively, politically, and fiscally feasible necessitated several steps. First, committees of Congress with responsibility for categorical legislation needed to agree to have certain rules or exclusionary features waived by the secretary when states gave assurance of their inclusionary intent. Second, several committees had to agree to having their own bills referred to the proposed piece of legislation. Third, these committees had to find the changes to their bills desirable. And fourth, the president's budget had to contain new dollars to provide the incentives to make the feeder bill work.

Soliciting feedback from HEW officials, Twiname (1971b) acknowledges that the idea of the feeder bill emerged as "a possible way to position existing categorical service authorities and meet the following goals: (a) enable states and cities to move toward service integration; (b) move towards revenue sharing and grant consolidation; and (c) find a viable alternative to the extremes of categorical legislation and comprehensive service legislation which would abolish categorical bills" (p. 1). The resultant bill was designed, therefore, to be independent of the categoricals, leaving intact their administrative authority as well as their responsibility to specify service goals, outputs, target groups, and funding levels.

Quite inventive for the time, the feeder bill proposed to allow governors and chief elected officials of general purpose local governments with populations of more than 250,000 to integrate the operations of human service programs in order to better deliver services to the consumer. Participation under the feeder bill would be optional, but those who elected to do so were required to produce, within two years, a plan for service integration. Such plans would be created by planning bodies established by the governors and chief executives and would provide assurances that existing levels of services would be maintained, that a needs assessment would be conducted, and that eligibility standards would be simplified. An explication of due process procedures and a description of how projects would be selected and how services would be provided were also required. Finally, the plan needed to identify the statutory and regulatory constraints that needed to be waived in order to integrate the planned services.

In addition to providing new dollars, the feeder bill planned to allow the reallocation of up to 20 percent of the money among programs in the feeder bill, pending the approval of a plan by the secretary. This 20 percent could also be used by a governor for discretionary projects that integrated services of the included programs. (An alternative of not restricting the percentage to be transferred was considered and dismissed.)

Many questions surrounded the feeder concept. Initially, it was uncertain precisely which programs should be included. Eligibility for the planning grants was discussed, as was the process of awarding grants and approving plans. Finally, there was concern over how the feeder bill would relate to the Family Assistance Program then under consideration.

The Allied Services Act of 1972

Though the feeder bill did not materialize, it proved to be pivotal in the thinking that emerged shortly thereafter in President Nixon's 1972 State of the Union address, wherein the Allied Services Act of 1972 was announced:

> The Allied Services Act, which will soon be submitted to Congress, offers one set of tools for carrying out the new approach [noncategorical, unified services delivery] in the programs of the Department of Health, Education and Welfare. It would strengthen state and local planning and administrative capacities, allow for transfer of funds among various new programs, and permit waiver of certain cumbersome federal requirements. By streamlining and simplifying the delivery of services, it would help more people move more rapidly from public dependency toward the dignity of being self-sufficient.
>
> Good men and good money can be wasted on bad mechanisms. By giving those mechanisms a thorough overhaul, we can help restore the confidence of the people in the capacities of their government. (Office of the White House Press Secretary 1972, p. 2)

The proposed Allied Services Act (ASA) of 1972 attempted (1) to strengthen human resources management and planning operations at the state and local levels (capacity building) and (2) to integrate human service delivery to meet clients' multiple problems (institutional reform). Specifically, the bill would allow governors to designate a state agency to develop a statewide allied services plan that would (1) designate statewide service areas, (2) select local areas to participate in the plan and designate a local agency to develop the plan, (3) select service types to be included in the plan, and (4) approve local service plans and their incorporation into a statewide plan.

The ASA would further allow the secretary of HEW, the state, and the local unit to consolidate planning funds extended by HEW and enable them to transfer 25 percent of federal assistance under HEW-assisted programs to other programs with an approved plan. It would also provide funding to meet the costs of the ASA: an estimated $20 million for the first year. Further, the secretary would be allowed to waive requirements related to statewide programs.

Notably, the legislation did not attempt to eliminate categoricals but sought a mechanism for coordinating them. In this sense it picked up the thinking of the feeder bill, but it also advanced it in specifying the categoricals that could be included in the ASA: Title IV-A and IV-B of the Social Security Act; Titles I, X, XIV, and XVI of the Social Security Act; Section 314(d) of the Public Health Service Act; Title V of the Social Security Act; the Vocational Rehabilitation Act; Title III of the Older Americans Act; Titles I and III of the Juvenile Delinquency Prevention and Control Act of 1968; Title XIX of the Social Security Act; Parts B, C, D, and E of the Community Mental Health Act; Parts C and D of the Developmental Disabilities Services and Facilities Construction Act; and the Adult Education Act. In short, it addressed child care; foster care; family planning; child abuse and neglect; child welfare; old age rehabilitative services; services to the blind and elderly; public health; maternal and child health; dental health; services to the disabled, to the mentally retarded, and to delinquent youth; alcoholism, narcotics, and drug addiction services; adult education; and facilities for the retarded and others with developmental disabilities.

Despite—or perhaps because of—its advances, the ASA raised concerns. Many people feared that the plan concealed serious intentions to cut federal expenditures for human services programs. Indeed, the 1972 State of the Union address focused on consolidation rather than expansion. Concerns were also raised regarding the planning process. The ASA called for gubernatorial designation of a state agency to lead the planning, but if a plan were to cut across categoricals and agencies, it was argued, the designated ASA agency should have the authority and capacity to integrate functions (Capoccia 1973). Further concerns addressed the governor's role in designating local service areas. Some minority groups have objected that the enlargement of gubernatorial discretion could dilute their own power and influence (Friesema 1969), and the ASA offered little inventive thinking around these sensitive issues. In fact, the ASA did worse: it did not specifically mandate input from community and other interest groups. The ASA came to be regarded as another setback for community groups who had striven to establish a viable role in community planning and delivery of services.

Another shortcoming came from a lack of ASA emphasis on professional preparation, a system as categorically fragmented as the programs themselves. Richardson's mention of the "guildmindedness" of workers found no expression in the legislation but raised concerns among critics. Well aware of disciplinary blinders, they seriously questioned whether such an integrated plan could ever be implemented by those dedicated to maintaining separate professional identities, guilds, organizations, and credentialing systems.

Moreover, concerns were raised regarding the relationship between the private and public sectors. The ASA did little more than require consultation among sectors; it did not begin to recognize the exemplary planning and coordinative work that had been accomplished in the private sector (Brooks 1971; Tropman 1971). This neglect reflected the division of the social welfare system, where much planning to that point had taken place largely in the private sector, with much operational responsibility in the public sector. If the ASA was to reframe that relationship, greater thought needed to be given to issues regarding the distribution of planning and operational responsibilities. (Recall the Mittenthal 1975 SITO analysis.)

Other concerns regarding the ASA involved the proposed $20 million allocation, an amount that was considered insufficient if a majority of locales were to be included in the effort. Using small dollars to drive a wedge into the enormous problems associated with vertical and horizontal fragmentation seemed functionally incongruous and fiscally inadequate.

Finally, an issue that would continue to plague service integration efforts was the question of regulatory flexibility. On the heels of the civil rights movement, with the real power of the poor in question, the inclusion of flexibility provisions was greeted with mixed reactions. Altshuler (1970) points out that the impetus for social change has been the result of establishing standards at increasingly higher levels of government and rarely—if ever—of local decision-making processes. For example, it was Congress and the courts who solidified changes in civil rights more than local governments. Indeed, some of those federal provisions and safeguards could be swept away by the relaxation of standards. The protection of service users could be minimized as standard and equitable delivery systems were excised from regulation, leaving arbitrary standards to determine service benefit levels and requirements.

Revamping the Allied Services Act

Feedback on the ASA poured forth as leaders in the field and the administration considered and reconsidered the proposed act. A conference at Williamsburg in November 1972 (Sprague 1972) resulted in additional analysis, as did the results of new data.

In September 1972 the Research Group and Kaplan, Gans, and Kahn (1972a) released its report on human resources in the United States, which attempted to take the experiences of six states as a data base from which to inform the ASA (Research Group et al. 1972a; see also Gans and Horton 1975). It examined the extent to which states consolidated human service functions, developed multifunctional planning and programming capacities (necessary to carry out the intent of the ASA), decentralized the service delivery system to uniform substate districts, and had in place the structure to provide the coordinated service delivery covered in the ASA. The report noted that states had taken considerable action in reorganizing their delivery systems via the creation of superagencies (p. 6). It indicated that such superagencies suffered from public skepticism because of their large scale and that in no case was public education administered in the same department—however large—as that providing social and other human services. On the positive side, the report noted that although the existence of such a superagency did not guarantee capacity for implementing the ASA, it provided an initial step toward service integration because it frequently built in a planning capacity. The report also observed that local capacity to develop such plans was limited and that there was little interaction between state and local governments.

In a frank set of recommendations regarding the ASA, the report noted the inadequacy of funding, the potential resistance that would be voiced by states against heavy local involvement in planning, the embryonic status of planning capacities despite the existence of the superagencies (which affirmed the need for technical assistance capacities), the differential time schedules that would be needed for planning in various locales, the need for measurable objectives and explicit work plans, and the need for a planned research agenda.

Significant in part because of its timing, in part because of its quality, the report affirmed the need to seriously reconsider the ASA. Ultimately the Allied Services Act of 1972 was withdrawn from Congress by the administration.

The Allied Services Acts of 1974 and 1975

After consultation with state and local government officials, the ASA of 1972 was revamped into legislation with three titles. The first title was explicitly noted as demonstration in intent and would provide authority for the secretary of HEW to make selected demonstration grants to the states to develop plans for the allied delivery of services. The governor was required to divide the state into human services areas, and the selected areas would create a plan to include public and private agencies. The plan would include an assessment of needs and take an inventory of resources to meet those needs, a description of programs to be involved, and procedures to engage multiple agencies. Dissenting views had to be submitted as part of the plan. The second title allowed for three-year implementation grants to assist in meeting the initial cost of consolidating services. Title 3 created five special authorities that would lend the necessary flexibility to make the ASA of 1974 a valid demonstration of service integration, including an evaluation component. The ASA also allowed the freedom to transfer up to 30 percent of HEW assistance monies from one program to another. In discussing the transfer provision before Congress, HEW under-secretary Frank Carlucci was careful to note its controversial aspects, calling attention to the sensitive issues regarding regulatory flexibility raised earlier:

> Some fear this provision is designed to enable wholesale shifts of funds now supporting a needed service to some other purpose, thus leaving a needy group without service and frustrating the intent of that service program. That interpretation is simply not correct. Rather the purpose of this provision should be taken in the context of all of the special authorities to permit integration of services and flexibility at the local level. Funds could not be shifted from services to more overhead. The national allocation of resources to particular programs could not be overridden at the state level. But localities which have heavier concentrations of needs in some categories as opposed to other localities could reflect that difference in the service they provide. (Carlucci 1974, pp. 11–12)

The ASA of 1974 was different from its predecessor in several ways (U.S. Department of Health, Education and Welfare 1974). As noted above, it tried to attend to mounting public concern regarding the flexibility/regulatory issue. It expanded support from two to three years, in accordance with the findings of the Research Group, and it increased the fund transfer provisions from 25 to 30 percent. The ASA of 1974 defined terms more carefully and precisely, including local service areas and human services. It recognized the need for some expanded technical assistance capacity at the federal level and the need to chronicle the activities that would be carried out under the act.

Despite these modifications, the Allied Services Act fell prey to proponents of categorical programs and did not pass Congress. Richardson (1976) notes that, for example, specific interest groups feared that service integration would permit the wholesale transfer of funds from one program to another, leaving the needy without services. Moreover, such integration could "dilute the unique experience and capabilities that each separate categorical program brings to bear" (p. 183). Redburn (1977) notes that seven state government representatives supported the legislation, but that opposition was expressed by the AFL-CIO, the National Education Association, the Advisory Committee on Venereal Disease of the American Social Health Association, the American Foundation for the Blind, and the National Rehabilitation Association. The National League of Cities and the U.S. Conference of Mayors also opposed the legislation in part because of its provision for state domination of human resources planning.

The bill was reintroduced in 1975 with some changes from the 1974 version (U.S. Department of Health, Education and Welfare 1975b). The 1975 version rescinded the requirement that governors divide each state into geographic areas coterminous with those of other service areas. Because this was a limited demonstration grant, a governor was required to designate only those service areas where a local demonstration would be mounted. The selection of the local sponsor became the responsibility of the local units or units of general purpose government after consultation with public and private providers. Moreover, the language specified that private not-for-profit agencies could be selected. A confidentiality provision was included, as was a mechanism for public disclosure and comment. Regarding the transfer of funds, the 1975 ASA provided that 25 percent of assistance monies could be shifted from program to program so long as the same target population was maintained. An additional 5 percent could be transferred without restriction. The 1975 act also eliminated transfer of funds from Title XIX of the Social Security Act and Title I of the Elementary and Secondary Education Act of 1965.

With these modifications, the proposed Allied Services Act continued to be debated, but support and enthusiasm waned. The challenges of garnering the requisite public support for a bill that threatened established ways of doing business, conventional disciplinary structures, and a categorical funding apparatus that had accorded visibility and rank to members of Congress made passage highly unlikely. Moreover, the Watergate scandal, the de facto disappearance of White House staff (S. Gardner, personal communication, November 1992), and personnel turnover all complicated the policy context, further derailing passage of the bill.

Rather than volumes documenting the torrid demise of the repeated ASA attempts, the absence of literature seems to suggest that it died with a whimper. But another explanation may be that rather than mourn the demise of the ASA, those committed to service integration applied their energies to a new strategy.

Title XX of the Social Security Act

Kahn and Kamerman (1992) note that "the 1975 enactment of Title XX, the first services Title of the Social Security Act, appeared to be an opportunity to develop a comprehensive, integrated delivery system for personal social services" (p. 10). The act, called the Social Service Block Grant, replaced social services funding to the states under several titles of the Social Security Act, namely Titles IV-A and VI. While maintaining the $2.5 billion funding ceiling previously established for Title IVA, Congress gave states much more flexibility in determining how social services dollars would be spent.

The Omnibus Budget Reconciliation Act of 1981 and Reagan's Twenty-four Block Grant Proposals

In the late 1970s and early 1980s, whatever conceptualizations of service integration had prevailed were recontoured significantly. First, rather than a focus on service integration as a means to improve service delivery, service integration became a means to reduce investments in human services. No one can doubt that President Ronald Reagan's zealous budget cuts marked the onset of a downward spiral of federal fiscal commitment. For example, real outlays expended on grants to state and local governments fell by 33 percent between 1980 and 1987 (Conlan 1988), while the real dollar value of Title XX Social Service Block Grants declined dramatically (Kimmich 1985). But even more significant, Reagan's "federalism reform" reshaped the substantive role of the federal government. Before and after becoming president, Reagan affirmed his commitment to a revamped federalism. Conlan (1988), quoting Presidential Assistant Robert Carlson, notes that federalist activities were "even closer to the heart of Ronald Reagan than the budget cuts" (p. 150). These federalist strategies took four forms: reducing and altering the priorities among grant-in-aid programs, proliferating block grants (24 during his administration), restructuring intergovernmental roles, and establishing regulatory relief.

While all are germane to service integration, the block grant strategy presents a clear picture of the difference between Nixon's and Reagan's approaches. The Nixon administration viewed block grants as worthwhile ends in themselves in that they would help streamline services. They were regarded as an efficient vehicle to combat excessive revenue increases *and* to capitalize on state and local expertise regarding services delivery. To Reagan, block grants were an effective means of weakening Washington control—a halfway house to total federal withdrawal (Carlson, qtd. Barfield 1981, p. 26). Nixon accepted higher spending levels for block grants, whereas Reagan typically cut funding levels.

The Omnibus Reconciliation Act of 1981 established nine new or revised block grants and simultaneously reduced the funding for the consolidated programs by 25 percent. The new block grants strengthened the role of the state, this time not so much at the expense of the federal government as at the expense of local nonprofit agencies, school districts, and small municipalities. States had fewer reporting responsibilities and greater discretion in spending their (albeit reduced) funds.

Though ostensibly catalysts for service integration, the block grant programs of the 1980s proved to do just the opposite. First, as Edelman and Radin (1991a) note, "fragmentation at the delivery end and block grants at the funding end are a perfect combination. Fragmentation reduces utilization and block grants weaken constituency support for funding" (p. 10). Second, bureaucrats, preoccupied with program survival, had little time and less concern for cooperative planning and service integration. In many ways, these efforts became sagas of failure that drained time and resources from the business at hand.

More optimistically, one can recount the history of service integration during this era, noting its contributions to another approach, via the use of categorical grants. It is to such a discussion that we now turn.

4

The Categorical Approach to Service Integration

Thus far, the discussion has focused on service integration efforts that, though generally lodged in HEW, have not had as their locus or impetus any single domain of practice or field of inquiry (such as health or education). Such a perspective is at once unfortunate and logical. It is unfortunate in that it yields a biased and somewhat delimited picture of the richness of service integration efforts from the 1970s to the present. And yet it is logical because most of the early efforts at service integration began with broad intentions that spanned disciplinary and categorical boundaries.

Because of the inherent challenges that the early initiatives faced, many service integration efforts of the late 1970s and early 1980s were launched from tighter disciplinary perspectives. Thus, as Kahn and Kamerman (1992) have pointed out, we see an emergence of discrete within-field efforts to integrate services across funding streams, as well as efforts launched from a single funding stream that attempt to envelop other services. These are quite distinct in impetus and flavor from the general service integration strategies described in the preceding chapters.

Scholars are divided on the overall viability of categorical initiatives to promote service integration. Proponents suggest that the utilization of categorical funding streams and the promulgation of within-field integration is a necessary prerequisite to cross-field and cross-funding integration. It is suggested that beginning from a categorical perspective does not necessarily wed or limit service integration efforts to a single field but offers a solid base for launching broader integration. Moreover, since the passage of comprehensive legislation is so complex, a categorical approach to service integration ensures that worthwhile efforts will not bog down in legislative inertia.

Other investigators suggest that categorical programs themselves are the barrier. How can change be advanced through the very structures that have historically impeded advancement? This school of thought regards categorical programs in any form as the problem, not the solution. Rather than taking a categorical program or a single discipline as the basis for integration, categorical integration efforts, it is thought, have served to *expand* a single domain—for example, creating a superagency. In such cases, services are not really being integrated; rather, the term *service integration* becomes a euphemism for program expansion or professional empire building. Gardner (personal communication, November 1992) suggests that often such approaches become little more than "robbing Peter to pay Paul. . . . What the victors call service integration everyone else experiences as a budget decrease." Indeed, efforts that masquerade as attempts at categorical service integration may be solipsistic initiatives that see themselves as the center of the world. Instead of reforming the system at the core, they amalgamate services under their own wings.

To be sure, categorical collaboration or categorical service integration efforts are increasingly abundant and controversial. The purpose herein is not to chronicle all such efforts or pass judgment on their efficacy. Rather, by examining some of the major categorically based efforts, texture and complexity can be added to the service integration kaleidoscope while providing additional vantage points from which to extract future lessons.

Child Mental Health

Service integration in child mental health is often dated from 1969, when the Joint Commission on Mental Health of Children issued a major report, *Crisis in Child Mental Health: Challenge for the 1970s*. The report noted that there was probably not a community in the nation that provided an acceptable standard of services for mentally ill children, and it set forth a comprehensive model of coordinated services for this population. It envisioned a multilevel child advocacy system with child development councils to work in local communities. Parallel authorities would coordinate the work of several regions, and state child development agencies would plan and coordinate services and programs within each state. At the federal level, a presidential council on children and a children's leadership agency were recommended. Coordination, comprehensive planning, and data collection were emphasized (Joint Commission on Mental Health of Children 1969). Echoing many of the themes of this report, the 1978 President's Commission on Mental Health called for a responsive social services system, featuring interagency liaisons, joint planning, and comprehensive case management (President's Commission on Mental Health 1978).

Spurred by these and other reports (Knitzer 1982), as well as by the work of advocates, one of the leading categorical efforts at service integration was launched in 1983 by Congress with an authorization of $1.5 million to the National Institutes of Mental Health (NIMH). The Child and Adolescent Service System Program (CASSP) was designed to improve service delivery to severely emotionally disturbed children and adolescents. Schlenger (1990; qtd. Kahn and Kamerman 1992, p. 15) notes its major goals:

—Improve the availability of continua of care for severely emotionally disturbed children and adolescents at the community level, and thus improve the availability and access to appropriate services across child service systems;

—Develop leadership capacity and increase priority for funding of resources for child and adolescent mental health services at both the state and community levels;

—Establish interagency coordination mechanisms and thereby increase levels of collaboration, and ultimately efficiency of service delivery among agencies;

—Develop family participation in the planning and development of service systems, treatment options, and individual service planning;

—Assure that service system development takes place in a context that is responsive to the special needs of culturally diverse ethnic minority groups;

—Develop the capacity for child and adolescent service system development and provide technical assistance;

—Evaluate the principles and practices of CASSP.

To achieve these goals, CASSP provides direct grants to states or mental health agencies to improve their mental health delivery systems. Though lodged in the mental health domain, the grants are explicit in their intent to integrate services across domains, including health, education, welfare, and juvenile justice. Like other programs, CASSP espouses no single model or approach but encourages diversity—what Richardson would have called capacity building (Kahn and Kamerman 1992). Moreover, to augment and chronicle the arrangements and outcomes, CASSP runs a technical assistance center at Georgetown University and has had extensive evaluation of its efforts.

Early CASSP evaluations noted that "an organized effort, an important challenge, and some outside funding can influence a state's system of care" (Kahn and Kamerman 1992, p. 15). Further, in the mental health domain, where services are characteristically bifurcated among the private and public sectors, the CASSP efforts have been particularly

The Historical Perspective

noteworthy in linking the two. But among CASSP's more important contributions has been the stimulation of a renewed attention to how children's services should be delivered. Knitzer and Yelton (1990), for example, suggest that a more rational system of service delivery might accord the child welfare field the protective role for individual children and give child mental health the responsibility of prevention and service expansion. Whether or not these are viable suggestions warrants consideration; that they are being offered suggests that one legacy of the child mental health engagement with service integration has been the reconceptualization of the entire system of delivery. Another result has been the affirmation that mental health care—though presently operationalized as a separate service or program that sometimes competes with mainstream services—must be an integrated component of multiple services. How best to achieve this goal remains unclear, but it is certain that the CASSP efforts will be influential as scholars and policymakers craft important alternatives.

Building upon the CASSP efforts, the Robert Wood Johnson Foundation launched a national demonstration program for youth in eight sites, with the goal of improving the management and delivery of community-based systems of care for disturbed youth. The focus of this intervention is not only to improve service delivery within the mental health field by providing models of service integration but also to construct durable financial mechanisms that might be replicable in numerous locales. By focusing on a piece of the service integration puzzle with a subfocus on inventive approaches to financing, these promising efforts may well yield strategic information that will lead to practical options for tackling the service integration elephant.

Finally, it is important to note that some advances in service integration have emanated from the judicial branch of government. *Willie M. v. Hunt* (1979) affirmed that children with serious mental health problems had a right to individualized treatment in the least restrictive environment possible. To implement the court decision, a review panel was established and an administrator hired. Building upon the 1969 report of the Joint Commission, the administrator advocated the establishment of a coordinated array of community-based services and place-ments. One of the key premises of the plan was the provision for linkages among the various components of the child service system. Despite difficulties in implementing the overall plan, two components advanced service integration work, notably the program of case manag-ers and the management information system. Soler and Shauffer (1990) note that "the Willie M. program is widely recognized as an important model for mental health services for children . . . a guidepost for developing comprehensive and coordinated services" (p. 287).

Health

Until recently, national efforts to encourage the integration of health services have been somewhat less robust than in other domains. Yet there has been a clear commitment to constructs allied to service in-tegration within health care, under the rubrics *community-centered, client-based, comprehensive, early identification, collaboration,* and *case management.* Further, within specific bureaus, projects of various sorts have been launched. For example, the Maternal and Child Health Bureau of the Public Health Service has, through a network of national resource centers, promoted a focus on coordinated community-based care for young children with special health needs. Special Projects of Regional and National Significance (SPRANS) sponsors demonstration efforts focusing on delivering coordinated health services to mothers and children, as well as on providing services to the handicapped. Healthy Start, a Bush administration initiative, was designed to reduce infant mortality by integrating health and education services. And the National Commission to Prevent Infant Mortality promoted one-stop shopping as a means of linking health and social services to meet the needs of pregnant women and their children.

Legislatively, the Maternal and Child Health Block Grant Program has been flexible enough to permit integrated services, but has not established sufficiently strong incentives to systematic service integra-tion. While adding flexibility, Congress—through the Omnibus Budget

Reconciliation Act (OBRA) of 1989—made service integration more of a priority by indicating that family-centered, community-based coordinated care was a purpose of the legislation, and provided funds for demonstration efforts that included service integration and home visiting. The legislation also required that coordinating mechanisms be established in the states to link Medicaid and Maternal and Child Health. Early and Periodic Screening, Diagnosis and Treatment (EPSDT), conventionally required for Medicaid-eligible individuals under age 21, was also revamped by OBRA to include greater emphasis on more comprehensive services, necessitating greater coordination across services—for example, child mental health care and Medicaid.

These important efforts underscore the intentions of the health field to consider service integration efforts. Certainly, countless efforts have taken root in localities and under the auspices of foundations. It is, however, noteworthy that though health care is a universal need and service, and thereby has the potential to serve as a nonstigmatized vehicle for integrating services, it has not done so with gusto to date (Kahn and Kamerman 1992). It remains to be seen whether the current health care reform movement will incorporate concerted attention to service integration.

Child and Family Services

The press for service integration in child and family services comes from two distinct sources, one private and one public. Private sector efforts to weld a cohesive system for children and families have taken many forms, responding in part to a paucity of federal leadership in this categorical area.

Among the most notable of the efforts to integrate services at the local level is a series of programs and strategies loosely identified as family support. Stemming from traditions that are characterized by their comprehensiveness and their tacit integration of services—settlement houses, self-support, parent support—family support programs are committed to serving the entire family, to preventing social problems and intervening before problems escalate, and to broad-based community engagement. These programs have developed primarily in the private sector. With program development free from regulatory constraints and the often burdensome guidelines that accompany federal dollars, family support programs have blossomed as hundreds of experimental laboratories, each tailoring its program and services to what does (and does not) exist within its community. In some cases, family support programs focus on young children as the point of contact with families. In other cases, the elderly are the contact point. Family support programs make their homes in churches, educational establishments, housing projects, community service centers, or community-based organizations established especially to offer family support services.

While family support programs have burgeoned, efforts among foundations have served as an additional impetus for communitywide service integration. Initiatives by the Annie E. Casey Foundation and the Pew Charitable Trusts have inspired the reorganization of child and family services in a number of states and communities. New initiatives are being considered by other foundations that have at their heart service integration for the improvement of a comprehensive array of child and family services.

In the public sector, the child welfare system has borne the brunt of criticism for inefficiency and a lack of systematic services. To stave off such complaints, a number of initiatives—some within the public sector and some mixing public and private streams—have been launched to improve direct services through an integrated approach, with the Homebuilders program and other family preservation efforts exemplifying this strategy. Alternatively, many efforts have begun to look more broadly at system reform for human services. Bruner and Flintrop, detailing the Iowa experience with decategorization, have been instrumental in advocating this systemic strategy (1991).

Leadership for systemic reform is being undertaken by governmental and professional organizations. In 1991 the secretary of health and human services established an Interagency Coordinating Council, with the goal of coordinating services and systems for children and families.

Much of the work to date has sought to link Maternal and Child Health and Medicaid. New efforts to expedite services to children and families are being introduced by President Bill Clinton and Vice President Al Gore as a part of their Reinventing Government strategy.

The American Public Welfare Association (APWA), long concerned about these issues, has also assumed a position of leadership. It has appointed a commission that has spent several years holding hearings regarding the structure of social services in the United States. Understanding that states differ widely in their organizational structures and in their commitments to such services, APWA has posited a three-tiered approach that has service integration at the core of each level: services for all families, services for families in need, and protective services for alleged abuse and neglect cases. In addition to this initiative, the National Association for Public Child Welfare Administrators and the State Mental Health Representatives of Children and Youth have also called for the development of a collaborative agenda and have offered a model for achieving it.

Diverse categorical collaborative efforts in the domain of child and family services have sought to link various efforts, including foster care, child abuse and neglect, teen pregnancy, child welfare, and protective services. In so doing, they provide an additional lens from which to view service integration, but one that does not yet allow us to see either a uniform picture or a clear path.

Child Care and Early Education

America's commitment to its young children has been episodic and fragmented, with various agencies, organizations, and sectors being engaged at different times in the delivery of services. A recent analysis by the National Research Council of the National Academy of Sciences, for example, notes that there are 31 programs in 11 federal agencies concerned with child care alone (Hayes, Palmer, and Zaslow 1990). Such fragmentation has been attributed in part to the following factors. First, for centuries public attitudes toward early care and education have been primarily framed by the hegemony of the home and the privacy and primacy of the family. Second, discordant public values regarding out-of-home nonmaternal care firmly rooted the financing of early care and education primarily in the private sector. Third, owing to a lack of public will and to robust philanthropic and private-sector involvement, governmental commitments were episodic, halfhearted, and typically targeted to children and families most in distress, thus permanently segregating both sponsorship (into public and private sectors) and participants (according to socioeconomic level). Fourth, when publicly sanctioned, early care and education efforts were handmaidens to widely divergent social missions, yielding a mixed array of governmental auspices and programs. And fifth, ambiguity of purpose and inconsistency of commitment yielded a lack of precision and cogency in defining and executing federal-state relationships (Kagan 1991). In short, ambiguity and inequity have characterized the development of highly segregated and fragmented services to America's young children.

In reviewing the history of early care and education in the United States, one is immediately struck by the need to place the struggle *among* programs within the context of the struggle *for* them. The development first of infant schools and then of day nurseries in the 1800s manifested the omnipresent value struggle between home and nonmaternal care (Cahan 1989). The result was "to establish poverty track educational institutions as practical alternatives to the traditional family-centered socialization process" (Tank 1980, p. 16). This pattern of poor children being relegated to public institutions was established early on and continues to characterize the field today.

This pattern continued with kindergartens, but service providers were expanded to include not only the schools but churches, labor unions, temperance groups, private businesses, and settlement houses, thereby fortifying the mixed-delivery system as a permanent characteristic of early care and education in the United States. And at the end of the nineteenth century as many more institutions began to serve young children, the fairly coherent ideology of an earlier time gave way to the varying goals and norms of the host institutions. But perhaps most significant, the response of government to young children became firmly ensconced: government's role was reactive, partial, and only legitimized as a means to a greater social end. As the twentieth century dawned, still without consistent federal involvement in early care and education, fragmented systems and ideologies and diverse quality reigned. With sad clarity, income segregation became synonymous with quality segregation: low-income children received low-quality services, high-income children high-quality services.

Motivated by the ravages of the Great Depression and by President Franklin D. Roosevelt's commitment to offer the American people a "new deal," Congress authorized funds to establish nursery schools so that mothers could go to work. The federal government's first foray into the field set several precedents. First, the quality of services was questionable. Second, because funds for the programs were funneled through the Federal Emergency Relief Agency (FERA), supported by input from the Children's Bureau, the command center was out of the hands of educators or specialists in child development. Though the need for educational input was acknowledged, it barely materialized, and its general absence hindered coordination among professions and organizations. At the federal level, child care was dispersed among agencies, with the Farm Security and Federal Housing Administrations also running programs. Funds for these efforts were short-lived.

Stimulated by another national crisis, World War II, the federal government entered the child care arena again under the aegis of the Community Facilities (Lanham) Act, administered by the Federal Works Administration (FWA), FERA's successor. Never fully sympathetic to the use of Lanham Act money for child care, the FWA was dubbed an agency "that never ceased to look ahead to termination of the program" (Steiner 1976, p. 17), a blatant acknowledgment of the federal government's tenuous commitment to early care and education. Not lodged in an agency with knowledge of or expertise in early education, the Lanham Act called for collaboration, in principle; but in reality, it made fragmentation inevitable.

From World War II to the civil rights era, women exercised their roles as homemakers, with children ensconced in the home. Federal concern for the plight of disadvantaged children resurfaced in the 1960s when a confluence of civil rights, education, and employment legislation led to the development of the Head Start program, the 1967 amendments to the Social Security Act, and a host of other isolated programs addressing the needs of children. Establishing a completely new funding apparatus and a structure that bypassed the states, Head Start was bred of mixed parentage—civil rights advocates and social scientists. Though inventive in design, Head Start remained programmatically removed from other early care and education efforts, despite a strong commitment to link with health and social service providers to enhance direct services offered to children and families.

While Head Start was growing, day care evolved on a separate track. Day care had been a part of the Social Security Act since 1962, but the 1967 amendments significantly broadened its authorization (Jackson 1973). On still another track, limited dollars were invested in early childhood education through the Elementary and Secondary Education Act (ESEA) of 1965. Title VII of the Housing and Urban Development Act provided support for child care centers, and the Model Cities legislation permitted day care expenditures amounting to about $9 million in 1971. Community Action Programs included provisions for preschool and child care services. Community Health Centers under NIMH allowed construction funds to be used to build child care centers. The Department of the Interior made funds available to American Indians for child care.

The mélange of efforts in the mid- to late 1960s yielded greatly increased services for low-income children and their families, to be sure. But the proliferation of early care and education activity during this era also marked a historical turning point with significant consequences for the early care and education system. Contrary to past practice, these federal involvements were to endure beyond other national efforts previously launched. Despite precarious funding levels and a number of attempts—some successful—to sweep away the enactments of the era, the 1960s efforts secured a permanent place in the federal pocketbook for nonschool-based programs for young children. Clearly, efforts of the 1960s and 1970s changed American early care and education, broadening it from a matter of private interest to one of significant public *and* private concern.

Such policy and ideological changes brought with them pervasive, though not necessarily unpredictable, practical consequences. First, as public preschool education was increasingly targeted to the poor, the income segregation that had characterized earlier efforts was fortified, becoming an immutable factor of early care and education. Second, the involvement of multiple federal agencies with scattered responsibilities exacerbated the problems of an already badly fragmented service delivery system. At the federal level, there was a lack of clarity regarding the relationships among the agencies that had responsibility for early care and education programs. The Children's Bureau, initially created to "investigate and report on all matters pertaining to the welfare of children and child life among all classes of our people" (Bremner 1970, p. 774), was perceived as "dinky, depressed, uninspired and uninspiring" (Steiner 1976, p. 39), certainly not up to the task of coordinating early care and education strategies or policies. Such lack of coordination and clarity at the federal level manifested itself at state and local levels as well, with dire consequences for child care accessibility, quality, and supply.

By the early 1970s, both the executive and legislative branches of government recognized the potential of collaboration, seeing it as a strategy that could help redress the fragmentation and inequity that plagued the early care and education field. In December 1967, Congress amended the Economic Opportunity Act (Section 522[d]) and called upon the secretary of the Department of Health, Education and Welfare and the director of the Office of Economic Opportunity to "take all necessary steps to coordinate programs under their jurisdiction which provide day care so as to attain, if possible, a common set of program standards and regulations and mechanisms for coordination at the State and local level" (National Academy of Sciences 1972, p. 1). Shortly thereafter, in April 1968, the White House proposed a Federal (Interagency) Panel on Early Childhood with responsibility to improve all early childhood programs financed by federal funds. Among its first recommendations was the establishment of the Community Coordinated Child Care (4C) program, the first federally initiated effort to coordinate early care and education. The intent was not to completely integrate all programs (although this was not prohibited) but rather to engender cooperative efforts by sharing services and staff, engaging in joint cross-agency training and visits, and establishing common programs where responsibility could be shared across sites. The concept rapidly gained visibility and popularity, so that by August 1971, 278 active 4Cs had been formally recognized.

The common perception is that the 4C program was modestly successful. Steiner sums up this view well: "Most attention was paid to coordinating matters of little importance probably because matters of great importance like day care program standards are inherently too divisive to permit coordination" (1976, p. 48). Such dissatisfaction was confirmed by Morgan, who attributed much of the problem to the "conflict between Washington and the regional offices" (1972, p. 7). With speculation about the value of the 4C program mounting, the National Academy of Sciences was asked to conduct an assessment of the program, the primary national assessment conducted by nonparticipants. More benign than the Steiner analysis but reflecting the Morgan concerns, the evaluation concluded that "4C represents . . . a sound concept as far as it went and one which, had it been properly implemented, might have made a major contribution" (National Academy of Sciences 1972, p. 32). The panel recommended that the federal government should encourage and support such cooperative efforts; but as it turned out, funding was gradually curtailed.

Some contend that the Comprehensive Child Development Act of 1971 included commitments to coordination and collaboration, though this is debatable. A cursory review of the bill considered by Congress indicates some sensitivity to the need for collaboration. At the federal level, it required the secretary of health, education and welfare to direct the Office of Child Development and the Office of Education to promulgate joint regulations to achieve coordination. Further, the secretary was authorized to prescribe appropriate regulations and arrangements to ensure coordination between Social Security and the Comprehensive Child Development Program. Dubbed an administrative monstrosity by some, an irresponsible promise by others, the legislation evoked lingering concern over issues of local control and coordination. After lengthy debate, a commitment to coordination, though not a strong one, made itself heard. Because President Nixon vetoed the bill, no one can know how such efforts might have fared. But a clear consequence of the veto was a diminution of advocacy for child care efforts in general and for collaborative efforts in particular.

Other legislation followed. The Child and Family Services Act of 1975, sponsored by Senator Walter Mondale and Congressman John Brademas, contained modest commitments to service integration in its call for the creation of a Child and Family Services Coordinating Council. But again there was no opportunity to test the efficacy of the council because the bill, like the Comprehensive Child Care Act before it, was brought down by strident charges regarding the professionalization of parenting and the "Sovietization" of America's children.

No more satisfactory was the fate of Senator Alan Cranston's Child Care Act of 1979. Designed to assist working parents, this legislation proposed direct funding to the states. Short-lived primarily because it lacked strong support from members of the Carter administration and the child care advocacy community (Levine 1982), the bill was withdrawn prior to a vote. Collectively, these three unsuccessful legislative attempts cast a pall over child care as a salable issue and eradicated legislative strategies to bring integration and cohesion to the child care field.

Nevertheless, despite the uncertainty of the times, the need for coordination remained strong. Growing numbers of working women, the sheer numbers of children in need of supplementary care, and the "demands for a conscious family policy" were all motivating forces for a more coherent approach (Grubb and Lazerson 1982, p. 217). Unable to wait for federal imprimatur, isolated communities set about the task of making child care arrangements more coherent through the development of information and referral systems (I and R's). Providing information to parents and acting as a fulcrum for activity in the child care field, I and R's helped stimulate linkages among services by giving technical assistance to new programs and family day care homes; by providing staff training and establishing employee clearinghouses for those wishing to enter the field; and by developing rich communitywide data bases that were later useful for significant advocacy efforts. The I and R movement gradually added services and expanded to become R and R's—resource and referral agencies. As the first sustained collaborative effort, these agencies form the heart of the collaborative tradition in early care and education.

Other strategies to unite the early care and education field evolved. Provider Service Networks (PSNs) represented a strategy that capitalized on local planning and broad-based participation of early care and education specialists. Designed to integrate individuals and organizations into a network, PSNs, when they functioned optimally, provided organizational assistance, either helping participating agencies to function more effectively or creating new organizations to represent the interests of providers. Less formal than other collaborative efforts, PSNs were an attempt to deal with the reality of interrelationships among individuals in the child care community and to optimize their interaction (Urban and Rural Systems Associates 1977).

Different from service integration as discussed thus far, partnerships between child care programs and schools were designed to provide direct services for children and families. Some of the child care programs were *housed* in public schools, some were *funded* by public schools, some were *staffed* with school personnel certified in education. Levine (1978) found that though stable funding was often perceived as a benefit of collocation in schools, none of the programs that he studied secured ongoing financial commitments from schools. Endogenous eligibility and housing patterns did little to alter the basic income-segregated system of early care and education. Although schools can be a viable repository for programs and services, their involvement can exacerbate an already inchoate delivery system. If these issues—including salary, benefit, and certification disparities—are addressed, however, school involvement can be a powerful force in redressing decades of fragmentation.

Finally, efforts to integrate services in early care and education have been advanced through Head Start and its related demonstration efforts, Head Start Planned Variation and Project Developmental Continuity (PDC). Results of the PDC effort indicated that Head Start–public school collaboration was a challenge in most of the communities, in spite of the additional resources provided by the project. Undaunted, the Office of Child Development launched other efforts to link Head Start and the schools, including Basic Educational Skills and, in the 1980s, a transition project. Not unexpectedly, many of these efforts required the establishment of local councils to advise the projects. In some cases, they were broadly constructed and served as catalysts of change within a larger community (Chapel Hill Training Outreach Project 1988).

In retrospect, it can be seen that scholars and activists of the late 1960s and 1970s recognized the complexities of the problems in early child care and education and set out with the best intentions to rectify them. Unfortunately, they were trapped in their own conceptual web: their solutions, like the system they were trying to save, were disorganized, idiosyncratic, and piecemeal. Too broad for such isolated responses, the challenge of collaboration was tacitly bequeathed, through legislation, to special education.

Special Education

The focus of massive legislative efforts and dramatic reform in recent decades, the field of special education provides particularly fertile ground on which to study service integration. The civil rights movement, which was instrumental in advancing the categorical programs in the 1960s, also left a legacy to families with handicapped children. No longer content to have their children isolated and receiving inferior services, parents of the handicapped mobilized to spearhead massive reform that brought with it new approaches to service delivery.

The reform called for action at two levels. First, a new, holistic view of rehabilitation led to the understanding that handicapped children, like their nonhandicapped counterparts, have multiple needs that are best addressed through a more comprehensive and individualized approach to service delivery (Brewer and Kakalik 1979; Katz and Martin 1982; Paul, Stedman, and Neufeld 1977). Second, the inhumane treatment that came to public attention via Willowbrook and the realization that all systems serving the handicapped were woefully inadequate, fragmented, and uncoordinated (Brewer and Kakalik 1979) brought into relief the need for comprehensive systemic reform.

One mechanism for reform was the Education for All Handicapped Children Act of 1975 (P.L. 94–142), which mandated that free appropriate public education and related services be made available by 1980 to all handicapped children between the ages of 6 and 18. (The law also established a default mandate of services for children in the age ranges of 3–5 and 18–21, but allowed states flexibility regarding these provisions.) Of immense import, P.L. 94–142 posed considerable challenges for the states and localities in many areas, including service integration.

From the outset, reports were circumspect about the potential of the legislation to achieve system reform. Elder and Magrab (1980) claimed that it caused havoc in the system of services to the handicapped. Brewer and Kakalik (1979) asserted that it was superimposed on existing federal special education programs without seeking to alter the system fundamentally. In part, such difficulties were wrought because, characteristic of the era, the legislation mandated a dramatic shift in focus from the federal to state and local levels. Although the work of some State Education Agencies (SEA) along these lines predated the law, the majority of SEAs suddenly found themselves front and center, bereft of the capacity and, in some cases, the commitment to what had heretofore been a more national effort.

Certainly, if the majority of states felt disfranchised from the process, the Local Education Agencies (LEAs), who were yet another step removed, were similarly ambivalent regarding their role in and commitment to the effort. From the beginning, universal state and local commitment to the legislation was tentative at best. Moreover, charged with the responsibility to carry out the intent of the legislation, the SEAS and the LEAS did not have the resources, visibility, or authority of many of the agencies already serving the handicapped (Rogers and Farrow 1983). They were caught in a classic dilemma: they had responsibility without authority and, in this case, without sufficient resources. Consequently, SEAS and LEAS were forced to build relationships with other, more powerful human service agencies to fulfill their charter (Elder and Magrab 1980; Rogers and Farrow 1983).

But achieving real service integration posed more challenges for public education than anticipated. Because of their historic autonomy, schools and local school districts were not natural collaborators. Professionalism, turf protection, and a captive market (via free schooling and compulsory attendance) are factors that have traditionally insulated schools from competition and cooperation with community services. As comparatively free-standing entities, SEAS and schools, when they have made linkages, did so only at the behest of other service agencies (Schenet 1982).

Structural disincentives to collaboration between education and human services are intensified by the division between human service administrators, who are accountable to the governor, and chief state school officers, who are either elected by the public or responsible to another entity (the state school board) not under gubernatorial control. They share neither authority nor accountability, making service integration more difficult to achieve.

It is not surprising, then, that after more than a decade of attempted linkages in special education, researchers concluded that despite great variation of efforts, on balance little collaboration among programs took place (Allington and Johnston 1989; Edgar and Maddox 1983; Helge 1984; Johnson, McLaughlin, and Christensen 1982; Katz and Martin 1982; Morgan 1985; Rogers and Farrow 1983; Schenet 1982).

Learning from this experience, and in an attempt to address shortfalls in the legislation, Congress enacted the Education of the Handicapped Act Amendments of 1986 (P.L. 99–457). The amendments established a new federal discretionary program to help states to develop and implement the coordinated system for handicapped infants and toddlers and their families—a departure from P.L. 94–142 in the age of children that the program serves and in the explicit attention it gives to service integration. In order to serve this population and shore up a failing system, the act specifically requires that states transform their fragmented delivery systems into comprehensive, multidisciplinary, coordinated systems (Gallagher, Harbin, Thomas, Clifford, and Wenger 1988). To achieve such coordination, the governor appoints a lead agency to coordinate the initiative. Interagency Coordinating Councils (ICCs) were legislatively mandated so that comprehensive planning and service delivery could take place across disciplines, governmental levels, and economic sectors.

It was clear that collaborative provisions were needed. Very young children typically demand a range of services—language and speech, physical development, health, and perhaps physical therapy—that spans sectors and institutions. To create the required Individual Family Service plans and meet other provisions of the legislation, practitioners would need to work across these sectors, necessitating some means of linkage that could be systematically engineered. Such a mechanism was essential because prior to this legislation, the bevy of federally funded state programs (Medicaid; Early and Periodic Screening, Diagnosis and Treatment [EPSDT]; Developmental Disabilities Block Grant; and Maternal and Child Health) had "never been required to share fiscal and programmatic responsibility for a single program, as they [were] required to under Part H of P.L. 99–457" (Pontzer 1989, p. 4). Moreover, the fiscal stakes are not insignificant: though begun with a modest authorization of $50 million for fiscal year 1987, federal funding reached $175 million in fiscal year 1992.

Armed with a legislative mandate, states have embarked on implementation activities with assistance from a national early childhood technical assistance system (NEC-TAS) located at the University of North

Carolina. Comprehensive plans have been prepared that include provisions for case finding, the coordination of data systems, a central directory, and collaboration. States are moving at different rates, with the ICCs playing various roles (Pontzer 1989). In some states, the ICCs are becoming catalysts for necessary reform. But Harbin and McNulty (1990) note that such success at the state and local levels is often hampered by the lack of service integration at the federal level. "Unless federal agencies are willing to tackle the problems of service eligibility, funding, and certification, the promise of service coordination may never come to fruition" (Harbin and McNulty 1990, pp. 48–49).

Kahn and Kamerman (1992) point out that P.L. 99–457 is an example of the "targeting of a *function* (early intervention and developmental enhancement) with an age *cohort* (infants and toddlers) . . . to develop a new structure around a program concept" (pp. 20–21). As such, it both reflects and anticipates categorical strategies to achieve service integration. Perhaps even more significant, the P.L. 99–457 effort reaffirms that, while working categorically from operational perspectives, we must be thinking holistically from policy perspectives.

Education

Recurring throughout the history of American public education, the call for schools to be integrated with communities and families dates back to the colonial period, when education was envisioned as a shared responsibility. Schools took the lead in the basics—reading, writing, and arithmetic—and families and the church, who were actually considered the primary educators, took responsibility for developing ethical character and vocational training (Cremin 1977). By the early nineteenth century, schooling had changed so dramatically that educators and communities were distressed by their common alienation from one another. Exacerbated by growing technology, the rise of professionalism, and the bureaucratization of the schools, the lack of school-family-community integration prompted the rise of countless reformers who were also concerned that schools were not fully meeting the needs of the new society. Women reformers—municipal housekeepers, as they were called—agitated for pure food, clean streets, and educational reforms that would help advance the overall well-being of poor urban youngsters (Reese 1978).

Concern about schools stemmed not just from the emphasis on the poor and on the new immigrants to America but from the demands of the middle class, who were intent on ensuring opportunities for their own children. The period from the 1890s to World War I witnessed the widespread tendency for parents from many socioeconomic groups to participate in school organizations that begged for reform and for better integration between home and school (Kagan 1987). In subsequent years, these groups played important roles in bringing into the school curriculum music, art, foreign languages, manual sciences, and domestic skills, as well as introducing school gardens, kindergartens, and health services. Indeed, the Women's School Alliance of Milwaukee provided school lunches in members' homes until it successfully agitated for a publicly funded school lunch program.

The Community School Movement, an organized effort to promote a broader community role for schools, took hold in the 1930s and rose to prominence in the 1950s. Designed to be a unifying force, community schools launched a number of initiatives that sought to link community services under the school aegis—adult classes, recreation programs, job preparation, and health care (Henry 1953). Recognizing their utility, Congress passed two acts that fortified support for the community schools concept: the 1974 Community Schools Act and the 1978 Community Schools and Comprehensive Community Education Act. Despite these efforts, the community schools movement in America remained somewhat circumscribed operationally, establishing itself in only about 10 percent of the nation's schools.

In the aftermath of the 1954 *Brown v. Board of Education of Topeka* school desegregation decision, communities demanded more control in the education of their young people. Such control ultimately coalesced into the community control movement of the 1960s that agitated for school reform from outside conventional school mechanisms. Alternatively, within school bureaucracies there were calls for more community responsiveness and for meeting the holistic needs of children and families (Seeley 1981). Title I of the Elementary and Secondary Education Act of 1965 had provisions for parent engagement and was somewhat permissive in its use of dollars for comprehensive and integrative services—a trend that was reversed in the 1980s. Since the 1960s, various legislative initiatives have sought to engage families and communities, most notably in the special education provisions discussed above. Moreover, schools have increasingly integrated services in areas that were once deemed the purview of the family: nutrition and health, adding mental health and counseling components. Indeed, the history of school reform in the United States is strongly linked to the history of the expansion of the public school's role beyond the formal schooling of the colonial days to accommodate a far broader definition of education.

With a somewhat flexible mandate, American public education, primarily because of its universality and its public funding—a characteristic not shared with other child and family services—became the linchpin of a continuing debate over service integration. On one side are those who firmly believe that the mission of the school should be broadly defined (to include comprehensive services) both because that is the responsibility of education as the nation's foremost socializing tool and because comprehensive services are what children need to thrive. The other side argues that the schools are already overburdened and dysfunctional; adding more responsibility, particularly without sufficient resources, is a social injustice that dooms American education to an even greater failure. In the middle are those who feel that some combination of positions can be achieved.

However imperfect, two terms, *school-based* and *school-linked*, help amplify this middle ground. Although scholars differ on precise definitions, advocates of school-based services suggest that schools should be the fiscal and physical home of services for children. They conceptualize them as "womb-to-tomb" service centers for children from age 5 to age 17. Some proposals also call for schools to be the locus of comprehensive services for children from birth to age 5. On the other hand, advocates of school-linked services press for a more collaborative strategy that allows various agencies to serve children and families, but to do so in a more integrated way. Both school-based and school-linked strategies call for service integration; the difference is that the former regards schools as the central, more powerful player in the integration and delivery of services, whereas the latter envisions schools more as equal partners with other agencies in the planning, integration, and delivery of services. It should be noted that although these two terms have sometimes been used interchangeably, as the service integration movement unfolds greater attention is being given to the more collaborative strategy of school-linked services, in which "(a) services are provided to children and their families through a collaboration among schools, health care providers, and social services agencies; (b) the schools are among the central participants in planning and governing the collaborative effort; and (c) the services are provided at, or are coordinated by personnel located at, the school or a site near the school" (Center for the Future of Children 1992, p. 7).

Models of service integration in schools are now blossoming across the country from Maine to California (Center for the Future of Children 1992). More than 800 such efforts have been chronicled by Joining Forces, a project that was cosponsored by the Council of Chief State School Officers and the American Public Welfare Association, with many leading to statewide legislation. (California, with its San Diego-based New Beginnings program and its numerous state-wide legislative initiatives—including S.B. 997 and Healthy Start—is particularly fertile.) Simultaneously, numerous efforts are under way to cross-fertilize information in the field, with the Department of Health and Human Services sponsoring a major technical assistance strategy. How-to volumes are proliferating, as are state-of-the-state reports. What is missing (though in progress) are firm evaluations of the efficacy of school-based and school-linked service integration.

Data available thus far, discussed in greater detail in subsequent chapters, affirm what much of the historical research has indicated: such efforts are extremely complex and time-consuming, irrespective of locus; they demand sustained, effective leadership and are highly vulnerable to contextual variegations (Bruner 1991; Kagan 1991; Melaville and Blank 1991; Morrill and Gerry 1990). It is noteworthy that renewed emphasis on service integration is taking hold more vigorously than in eras past and is beginning to be accepted as an integral part of the school reform movement, not merely as an add-on strategy.

Presently many service integration initiatives are state- or locally based categorical efforts, reversing the trend of the more nationwide, noncategorical efforts of the 1970s. Many of the more recent efforts, though launched from a categorical base, attempt to become more comprehensive over time. In addition, through clearer and more circumscribed goals, many have the benefit of being more family-centered and outcome-oriented than their predecessors of past decades. Nonetheless, there is reason for caution, since such a categorical approach can open the door to agency aggrandizement instead of collaboration, with entrenched turfism driving categorical expansion rather than true integration. Further, the lack of a master plan uniting these categorical efforts can result in multiple overlapping initiatives, further fostering the very fragmentation they were created to eliminate.

Part II
The Theoretical Context for Service Integration

5
Evolving Definitions

The long and varied history of service integration has seen incremental advances in our understanding of this reform strategy and our facility with its implementation. Although the focus of much attention and thought, however, a clear and agreed-upon definition of service integration has remained elusive. Virtually every study, piece of legislation, book, or policy statement has commenced with its unique definition. Like a kaleidoscope reflecting subtle variations with each twist of the armature, the term takes on slightly different connotations each time, though they all bear a strong resemblance to one another. The resemblance was especially obvious in the early days, when the definitions lacked precision. Today, as multiple definitions abound and undergirding assumptions vary, it has become harder and harder to reach agreement on the meaning of service integration. Despite this lack of agreement, there is growing sophistication regarding the activities and premises that constitute service integration. To truly understand the concept, one must step back and examine its different rationales and the tenacious struggle to reach definitional consensus.

Different Rationales of Service Integration

The cacophony of definitions of service integration emerged in part from historical circumstances that framed the structure of service delivery: burgeoning categorical programs, overlapping geographical and political jurisdictions, and evolving constructs of federalism, to mention a few. But these structural ambiguities also derived from a far greater problem—the absence of clarity regarding the basic purposes of American educational and social service institutions.

Wavering between being an agent of social reform or a defender of the status quo, America's educational and social service institutions vacillated with each reform as to their fundamental raison d'être. Such ambivalence of mission is noted in the literature, with Brager and Holloway (1978) suggesting that organizational tension emerges as a result of such ambivalence. They suggest that "in no other sector of the society is this more the case than in the human services" (p. 3). Affirming such ambivalence, Rein notes that the "goals of social services are varied; they serve many masters, including social control. They are not simply 'humanitarianism in search of method' as has been suggested" (Cohen 1958; qtd. Rein 1970, p. 104).

Such turbidity of purpose has been dubbed the most elusive and intractable issue in the social services (Rein 1970, p. 105). In part, this is the case because we assume that any analysis of problems—a prerequisite for defining what needs to be altered—is predicated on a clear understanding of purpose. How can we define an ameliorative construct like service integration if we are not certain of what the basic conditions of effective systems should be?

Reflecting this inherent dilemma, Rein (1970) begins not by attempting to define service integration or to delineate its goals, but by articulating the problems such reforms hope to address. He contends that most reform efforts are directed at one or more of four persistent problems in the organization and distribution of social services: (1) the dispersal of similar functions (duplication of effort); (2) discontinuity of related functions (occurring when many community agencies share the same clientele over time); (3) incoherence when different functions are pursued with no relation to each other; and (4) consumer choice—a special issue when there are alternative programs to reach a similar aim (Rein 1970, p. 105). To rectify these problems, Rein—anticipating the potent definitional work that was to come—identified various types of linkage:

> The problem of dispersal calls for strategies which rely on cooperation of *personnel.* By contrast, discontinuities require coordination of *policies* among related functions to achieve some defined outcome, and incoherence calls for coordination of policies among unrelated programs, for which no single overarching goal or outcome can be specified. Constrained choices require greater freedom to select among alternative *programs,* by both present or future service users. Each problem in the organization of services thus implies a different target for action. No one pattern of reorganization is likely to solve all the problems presented. (p. 134)

Taking a similar tack that begins with a problem analysis, Agranoff (1977) offers a broad set of rationales that simultaneously predict the need for service integration and frame the essential elements of its definition. He suggests five trends that make service integration essential. First, the expansion of categorical programs—with their isolated response to isolated problems, their entrenched independent human service establishments, and their functional specialists—has precipitated the need for a more integrated approach, one that reflects the integrated reality of clients' lives. Second, he discusses changes in the roles of government that have led it to operating, purchasing, regulating, and funding efforts, consequently obfuscating its overall role. This impetus for service integration relates to an escalating lack of clarity regarding government's differentiated functions—what Osborne and Gaebler (1992) refer to as steering versus rowing roles. Inclusive, the third rationale cited by Agranoff relates to various recognized service delivery problems: fragmentation, discontinuity, inaccessibility, and unaccountability. Fourth, Agranoff suggests that the lack of goal attainment further necessitates service integration. Finally, he cites a fresh desire by government officials to put programs into some coherent policy framework (Agranoff 1977).

Agranoff was clearly articulating the multidimensionality (and even the language) of need that reverberated through Richardson's equally general delineation of rationales for service integration, set forth in a 1971 memo: "developing an integrated framework within which ongoing programs can be rationalized and enriched to do a better job of making services available within the existing commitments and resources. Its objectives must include such things as: (a) the coordinated delivery of services for the greatest benefit to people; (b) a holistic approach to the individual and the family unit; (c) the provision of a comprehensive range of services locally; and (d) the rational allocation of resources at the local level so as to be responsive to local needs" (Kaplan 1973, p. 3; qtd. Agranoff and Pattakos 1979).

Other rationales reappear in the literature: increasing the effectiveness of service delivery, raising its efficiency or its economy, and enhancing its accountability. Gans and Horton (1975) amplified the intent. *Effectiveness,* in the government's terms, refers to the responsiveness of government, at all levels, to consumer needs in ways that can be clearly evaluated. *Efficiency* implies economies associated with service integration (reflecting Richardson's statement of improving service availability within existing resources). In this sense, efficiency constitutes both a rationale and an end product of service integration. Finally, *accountability* refers to local general purpose governments and to the general public rather than to service providers or consumers.

In reviewing these rationales, Gans and Horton suggested that perhaps they could be condensed into two. First, *availability* of services to clients who need more than one service is enhanced if the services are coordinated. And second, *efficiency* in the delivery of services to clients is greater if delivery is integrated rather than fragmented. The Gans and Horton delineation of rationale—one that stressed availability and efficiency—served as the basis for their detailed and well-regarded investigation, as well as for many studies that followed. As such, the availability-efficiency construct has become prominent in the literature and in much of the thinking surrounding service integration.

This construct, interestingly, evaded quality of service as a primary rationale. The focus was on availability (which the authors further defined as accessibility and continuity) and efficiency (which includes the elimination of duplication of services and the realization of economies of scale). So, although considerable attention has been devoted to the availability-efficiency rationale, little in the early definition of service integration was directly related to considerations of the quality of services as a discrete factor.

Moreover, beyond the lack of attention to the quality of services themselves, little in the early rationales directly addressed qualitative improvements (direct outcomes) in the lives of children and families. Indeed, this failure may be attributed in part to the lack of a direct-outcome orientation in the service systems themselves. As noted above, the raison d'être of human service systems, although never precise, was built on the premise of problem eradication, not on a clear, specific rationale based on client-oriented goals. In part, then, the ambiguity of purpose in human services in general may have also contributed to the lack of clarity regarding the rationale for service integration.

From Rationales to Definitions

Given the complexity of its origins and the many rationales for its existence, service integration has waffled without clear definition for decades. The problem was noted in an early report on service integration: "Service integration is still an evolving art about which little is known. . . . The very term 'service integration' does not have a generally

Evolving Definitions

accepted meaning" (U.S. Department of Health, Education and Welfare 1976, p. 3).

Sometimes service integration was referred to as an objective (an integrated framework) and sometimes as a process (creating integrative linkages). In the early days of HEW, the process definitions seemed to be used more frequently, perhaps tacitly implying acceptance of the above rationales and objectives. Within HEW, the term began to mean the process by which two or more categorical programs were linked. Though applied and accepted, this definition was somewhat narrow in that (1) it concerned programs with mutually compatible objectives, service elements, or client groups, (2) its use was generally restricted to HEW and did not routinely include other departments, and (3) it was process-oriented (Gans and Horton 1975).

As service integration work began to evolve, this definition—the process by which two or more categorical programs are linked—was found to be somewhat constraining, and so it was quickly altered for the Gans and Horton study to mean "the linking together by various means of the services of two or more service providers to allow treatment of an individual's or family's needs in a more coordinated and comprehensive manner" (Gans and Horton 1975, p. 32). Although including a larger number of HEW programs and services, this definition excludes a single agency's linking services from two or more categorical grants unless that agency united two previously independent entities. It also leaves out of the definition recipients of comprehensive grants that were designed to render multiple services.

Other attempts to define service integration entered through the back door, defining service integration by explicating its strategies. They offered explanatory definitions that were distinguished, on the one hand, by the techniques of service integration—collocation, joint funding, shared management information systems, and coordinated program planning—and, on the other hand, by domains—core services, advocacy, administrative functions. Others conceptualized the vast array of efforts taking place under the rubric of service integration as everything from building comprehensive systems to enacting procedural changes (Mittenthal 1975). Complicating the panorama, the question of intralevel and interlevel governmental approaches to service integration differentiated between horizontal and vertical integration.

A helpful distinction was offered by Redburn (1977) when he noted that throughout the literature two basic aspects characterize existing approaches. The first refers to structural arrangements or administrative techniques that eventuate in changes in government generally and in the organization of government agencies that administer human services. It incorporates efforts by municipalities, states, and regional agencies to share authority across agencies, to create super- or mega-agencies, and to engage in joint planning and evaluation across systems. The second aspect refers to the nature of the services and their delivery mechanisms. This includes efforts to improve direct services, case management, client planning, client diagnosis and referral, and so forth. Though not precisely the same, similar bifurcated definitions that distinguish between service delivery and system change approaches have been offered by others (Agranoff 1974; Gans and Horton 1975).

However tidy such definitions appear, a lack of definitional consensus persisted, producing an array of operational consequences. First, the two different approaches—service and system—have been confounded in the eyes of practitioners, policymakers, and researchers, resulting in the implementation of mistargeted strategies. Second, often a causal relationship has been implied—that is, service change (presumably service integration) is contingent upon system change. Third, and more positively, the lack of definitional clarity has resulted in a broader constituency for service integration. Redburn (1977) notes that this bifurcated definition has relevance for direct service providers and groups wishing to extend their management control. Using a single term for both approaches, however, obfuscates accountability, making it difficult to determine when service integration has been accomplished. In retrospect, it seems that the Redburn analysis is correct. A broad definition enabled the amassing of a larger constituency for service integration, thereby serving the policy agenda, at least initially. But because the definition did not presume to specify accountability modes or norms, evaluation was rendered less effective, perhaps eroding political support for service integration.

A Comprehensive Definition

As work on service integration evolved, so did the need—and prospects—for a more refined definition. Workers in the field began adapting the construct to fit new situations, as did policymakers, so that examples of different kinds of service integration efforts proliferated. Conversely, changes in the bureaucracy made it apparent that not all efforts were designed precisely to address the original rationales for service integration, but that service integration was sometimes a byproduct of their attempts to achieve other goals.

Armed with fresh examples and a growing conceptual base, Agranoff and Pattakos (1979) compiled the most thorough definitional and conceptual approach to service integration that had existed. They divided their framework into four essential dimensions, cautioning that the dimensions are and should be synergistic: (1) service delivery, (2) program linkages, (3) policy management, and (4) organizational structure.

Agranoff and Pattakos (1979) suggest that integration at the service delivery level is grounded in the ideological orientation and values of the service provider. It regards clients as complex individuals with multiple needs, which must be addressed by a multidisciplinary approach that encourages the provider to engage in many different strategies and to invoke many services. Such a perspective is seen as holistic and acknowledges that client problems generally are intertwined and cannot be remedied as discrete needs. The authors suggest that this dimension may be independent of the policy process because such client-level integration can take place often without policy alterations. The primary mechanism related to this dimension is case management, in which the client is assisted in designing and executing a coordinated plan of services.

The rationale for this dimension emanates directly from the turbulence of the 1960s and its eventual manifestation in the New Federalism. More explicitly, such changes were accompanied by the empowerment of clients and their conversion in human service thinking from dependents to consumers or constituents (Gilbert 1970), capable of choice and taking an active role in problem identification and solution. The emergence of the self-help and family support movements contributed to the realignment of professional roles, fostering greater flexibility, less reliance on professionals, and greater appreciation of the generalist roles. The debunking of the medical model through holistic approaches to health care and the community approach to mental health care also supported the movement toward integrated services at the point of delivery.

According to Agranoff and Pattakos (1979), the second dimension, program linkages, is the central focus of many service integration studies in that it attempts to link discrete services into a multifaceted delivery system. It links autonomous agencies so that their activities can be blended in service to consumers: "Program linkages are the means by which two or more independent agencies cooperate to smooth out the non-service delivery approach aspect of services without affecting the policy decisions and policy statements from which the programs operate" (p. 40). They change the way agencies interact with one another, but typically do not modify the frontline experience of workers or consumers. Often this dimension functions independently of the organizational structures because it deals with relationships among independent structures and is not concerned with restructuring or organizational changes within a single organization. Program linkages do not guarantee improvements in service delivery or in client outcomes. Examples of program linkages include shared information systems (including information and referrals), collocation, and the creation of decision-making groups to conduct joint planning and budgeting.

Program linkages are the clearest outgrowth of the fragmented history of human service policy. Their precedents are in the nineteenth-century charity organizations and in the United Way, in particular its mobilization and planning functions. More recent variants include community action agencies and some of the Model Cities efforts.

The third dimension is policy management (Agranoff and Pattakos

1979). It represents efforts of the general purpose government to unite program strands to increase the coherence and responsibility of the human service system, especially in the light of greater public demand for and involvement in human services. Policy management activities may be seen as one type of capacity building. The core of policy management lies in its function to "assess needs, set priorities, make allocative judgments, foster a particular course of action, and monitor outcomes, with a *problem,* not a program-by-program orientation" (p. 80). Such capacity requires a wider, multilevel perspective, best achieved by general purpose government, which is above categorical boundaries that divide human services and is responsible to the public interest. Policy management depends on the ability to conceptualize policy not as a discrete variable but as a comprehensive, continuing course of action. Policy management activities involve the creation of groups (committees, councils, task forces) to conduct policy-level needs assessments, set policy priorities, and monitor the service system. Funding strategies, including the provision of "glue" money for a service integration infrastructure, refinancing services with federal funds, and the decategorization of funding streams, are related reform activities in this domain.

The policy management dimension is the least considered in service integration, in part because it is a comparatively new construct, and in part because policy management is costly and politically volatile. Fluctuating economic and political climates, as well as state restrictions on the authority of substate units, have also impeded the full development of this dimension.

Policy management has weak links to service delivery, though by opening up human services to public scrutiny, it can be a catalyst for changes in provider attitudes, facilitating program linkages via the creation of interagency mechanisms. Moreover, it is a powerful impetus to such linkages, given its role in identifying goals and gaps in the overall system and its allocative function.

The fourth dimension is organizational structure (Agranoff and Pattakos 1979). This dimension refers to the reorganization or creation of government structures to support and facilitate the other three dimensions. It includes unifying linkages among formerly independent organizations and the consolidation of organizations. The primary example of this dimension is evidenced in the organization of agencies and their reorganization into super- or mega-agencies, such as state human service agencies. This dimension is only weakly joined to service delivery but is intimately aligned with policy management in that it fosters coordination functions, joint planning and evaluation, and the development of joint councils.

The Agranoff and Pattakos definition, though not ideal, is comprehensive and practical. Although it should not be considered impervious to modification, it does clearly delineate the different rationales for and visions of service integration. Clearly, multidimensionality characterizes the terrain, and this definition is viable in that it accommodates both domain disaggregation and the interrelationships of domains. Moreover, it enables architects and analysts of service integration to understand that each domain, though attempting to wrestle with the same constructs of fragmentation and inaccessibility, does so from different perspectives that lead to different strategies.

For example, all four domains are concerned, directly or indirectly, with the improvement of client outcomes, but given their different assumptions, they execute their work differently. The service delivery domain wants to improve services directly, by circumventing a focus on systems change. Acknowledging systemic flaws, this domain focuses on the client as the unit of intervention and works around the system to integrate its services. The program linkages domain accepts the existing fragmentation as a given artifact of a pluralistic American political and governmental system. It too does not attempt to create a new alternative. Rather, it works within the existing system to strengthen the relationships between fragmented programs; its unit of intervention is the program. The policy management domain also recognizes the fragmentation of the system, but seeks to alter it by creating and contouring policies. Its unit of intervention is the policy apparatus with which it attempts to change basic patterns of policy-program interaction. This domain is the most volatile of the four and is often subject to economic and political vicissitudes. Nonetheless, investing energy in this domain has politically high payoffs. Finally, the organizational structure domain assumes that change is necessary, and that such change is warranted for its efficiencies and economies; it also assumes that change initiated at the top will ripple through other layers of the service integration network. It is a top-down model of change, with the unit of intervention being the bureaucratic organizations that typically have administrative responsibility for human services at the state and sometimes substate levels.

We accept the Agranoff and Pattakos distinctions, if not precisely their labels. In the future, service integration needs to be consistently subdefined so that these distinctions are clear and gain widespread acceptance. Moreover, alternative terms—driven more closely by the unit of intervention—might explicate the differences that the authors intended. The Agranoff and Pattakos concepts could benefit from a crisper and more unified set of labels: client-centered integration, program-centered integration, policy-centered integration, and organizationally centered integration. Relabeling the domains so that the terms more clearly reflect the *locus* and *focus* of the service integration strategies herein described provides a suitable structure for the discussions in the following chapters. Moreover, by eliminating the words *services* and *systems* from any of the specific domain labels, we allow that all domains may be engaged in the improvement of systems through service integration strategies.

Although they add greatly to definitional and conceptual understanding, these definitions may not translate as discrete entities into the world of practice. Indeed, countless service integration efforts have blended work across domains. It is not the intent of the originators of the domains, anymore than it is ours, to suggest that any one domain is the more significant or preferred. Rather, it is to suggest that different domain emphases will yield different results, all of which must be evaluated with far greater precision than amalgamated definitions have permitted thus far. Using the domains as guideposts for understanding, implementing, and evaluating service integration is the challenge we all face.

6

Multiple Theories

The preceding discussion suggests that an evolving literature has lent precision to a theoretical definition of service integration. It should be noted, however, that such theoretical clarity does not necessarily pervade the practice literature and that such conceptual refinement did not emerge overnight. Rather, it has evolved from numerous reiterations of analysis over time, many of which were themselves extruded from evolving theories in allied disciplines.

Not a recognized discipline itself, service integration owes its intellectual genesis to many disciplines, each of which has contributed varying ideas and approaches to this theoretically neoteric field. In this chapter we examine some of the theoretical formulations that have contributed to service integration as we know it today, teasing out the conceptual antecedents of service integration and paying particular heed to literatures on intergovernmental relations, organizational theory and behavior, and systems management and change. The chapter is not intended to be a comprehensive review of multiple, vast disciplines, but instead focuses on selected theories related to structuralist, humanistic, and systems approaches to change.

Organizational theory has been likened to a game of chess, with coordination the king, the most difficult to capture (Gulick 1937), and with moves on the board, particularly the early ones, directly determining the resulting character of the game. How one perceives the character of service integration directly determines how one manages the game. Three theories predominate. The first is rooted in the *structuralist* tradition and suggests that lack of coordination is first and foremost an issue of structure, of how organizations are built and organized internally. The second perspective is more *humanistic* and holds that service integration is largely a function of the behavior of individuals who conspire to make up an organization. From this vantage point, the key ingredient of service integration is the relationships among individuals, how they balance power and how they behave. This perspective includes the behaviors of individual categories of people—providers, clients, managers, policymakers—and their interactions in the collective behavior of organizations. The third perspective focuses on *systems* and suggests that service integration is most appropriately viewed as the intent of an organization or series of organizations, through enlightened management strategies, to deal with issues relating to the external environment. Systems theory suggests that when subunits of an organization are conceived as totally linked entities, and when they deal with issues of equilibrium and stabilization, the organization will be able to realize its stated purposes.

Each of these broad approaches is supported by theoretical literature and specific taxonomies. Again, like the Agranoff and Pattakos dimensions discussed in chapter 5, each theoretical perspective, though presented here independently, is linked in the minds and actions of service integrators, with individuals having varying predispositions toward the three perspectives.

The Structuralist Perspective

Advanced by Gulick and Urwick (1937), the structuralist view in its earliest construction espoused a top-down theory of administration that subjugates the individual to the purposes of the organization. Organizational goals are defined, individuals are hired, work tasks are delineated, and authority lines and structures for managing authority and coordinating activities are created. Assuming a functional dichotomy between politics and administration (Harmon and Mayer 1986), division of work became a primary mode in the organization of public service activities. Efficiency became the goal.

The structuralist approach, though seemingly arcane, influenced early thinking and teaching in public administration for half a century. Many familiar and long-exalted "proverbs" grew out of this approach: do not supervise too many people; establish unbroken lines of authority; group like functions together under a single command. Such a structuralist perspective also legitimated an endless shuffling of the boxes, a superficial reorganization strategy that has been widely used as a substitute for more genuine service integration. Though many of these concepts and efforts have long since been disregarded, the early work, modified by Simon (1976) and others and ultimately augmented by the humanist approach discussed below, created a theoretical context in which organizational elements reigned and in which early approaches to service integration were considered.

Emanating from an entirely different and somewhat contradictory perspective, another set of theoretical assumptions also undergirds the structuralist orientation. Rather than exalting the organization, this line of thinking disparages the efficacy of organizations in executing their functions. It suggests that many human service organizations—and welfare organizations in particular—operate in such a way as to support and sustain poverty. Gerry (in press) notes that the eligibility requirements that enable access to categorical programs are perverse. Premised on medical need, economic unworthiness, and unproductiveness, they thus serve to stigmatize and disempower individuals. Whether they were intended to do this or not, the system is so dysfunctional as to perpetuate if not accelerate dependency. Such an orientation clearly lodges the lion's share of the responsibility on institutions, not on the individuals they serve. In this interpretation, social Darwinism and the attribution of poverty to biological factors yield to a reexamination of structural factors in the bureaucracies that the poor—who are given little choice—are forced to navigate.

These two distinct lines of thought share a heuristic approach for understanding how organizations are driven. They suggest that the primary lens for regarding the functioning of human service organization is shaped by structural considerations.

Relating Area and Function

Though not impervious to change, structural variables are durable characteristics that frame basic interactions and approaches to organization. Recognizing the pervasiveness of such structural regularities enables analysts to understand why solutions are so elusive, why tensions are bound to exist, and therefore why service integration will inevitably be perpetuated as a domain of inquiry and as a goal.

Most fundamental among the structural regularities are the variables of area and function, which inherently compete in any organizational structure. Not a contemporary phenomenon or one restricted to the United States, the challenge of dividing up organizations so that they are effective—what Gulick and Urwick attempted to do—is ubiquitous and necessary. The problem is that we are forced to select between vertical functions and horizontal areas as the basic organizing units— two decidedly different ways of breaking up the parts of an organization. Fessler (1973) has noted that the functions may be regarded as vertical planes that transcend horizontal areas. For purposes of our discussion, vertical functions are the disaggregated planes that make up the human service spectrum—health, education, social services, mental health, and so forth. In contrast, areas are horizontal planes that embrace all the functions. In our case, these areas refer to various levels of government. Individuals engaged in the same functions will share interests and concerns regardless of their area or level of government. One such shared interest may be protecting their functional domain from encroachment by others; another might be advancing the standards of their functional domain. Functional domains outside of government are another important design element, including the evolution of professional organizations, unions, and other nongovernmental alliances.

In simpler eras, when the basic organization of American society was crafted, there was an assumption of tidiness—that is, that a functional domain would attend to its charge, which would be the responsibility of a single organization, not parceled out among several agencies. Similarly, tacit expectations were held for each level of government, pending modest fluctuations in federalist approaches. The operative principle was that as much responsibility as possible would be lodged at the level of government closest to where tasks were executed. Inevitably, national security was left to the federal government, and localities were responsible for day-to-day affairs. Such a structural approach is no longer viable for human services—if it ever was—because the problems being addressed cross structural boundaries of both function and area. Human service delivery, from the structuralist perspective, is caught in a dilemma: it is forced to deal with an arcane frame that is no longer suitable for the human service picture it has been designed to encase.

The result is that cosmetic solutions have been tried. Informal arrangements, councils, intermediate levels of government, and intermediaries have been established to combat the inefficiencies of the area/function dichotomy. Though marginal in effectiveness, such efforts to reduce both area and functional parochialism have yielded important knowledge. First, we understand that the least cooperative government or functional agency "fixes the threshold level of cooperation for all participants" (Fessler 1973, p. 9), a fact that suggests why structural entities are hard-pressed to advance service integration efforts either rapidly or fully. Second, we understand that even when such efforts work, they tend to succeed with the "easy" problems; Fessler notes that the nation has not been blessed with many examples of institutional cooperation or service integration that have solved hard problems. Fessler, though not very optimistic, offers a structural solution: the dual or matrix supervision system, wherein function and area both form domains of engagement and supervision.

Of great interest, the matrix approach to structural organization and supervision was also advanced by Curtis (1981) after reviewing a number of efforts to launch and sustain service integration efforts. Examining the ways communities consolidated and allocated power, Curtis concluded that the matrix model had the benefit of offering two worldviews simultaneously. He notes that these worldviews concern geographic areas and subareas of the community and specialized functions of professional services. In this approach, as in most matrix structures, workers report to two bosses, one within the area and one within the function. Such collaborative supervision opens the door to the sharing of power and resources, necessary ingredients to several of the service integration dimensions discussed in chapter 5. Curtis notes that the matrix model, in contrast to multiservice centers or mediated models, provides opportunities for greater worker self-initiative, greater flexibility in day-to-day work, and greater worker responsibility. Moreover, organizationally the matrix approach to structuring the delivery of services leads to greater experimentation not typically associated with bureaucracies.

Linkages among Agents of Government

A second strand of structural theories emanates from concerns specifically over the relationships between levels of government. The field of intergovernmental relations (IGR) remains imprecisely defined. Its origins go back to work by Snider (1937) and Anderson (1960), though Graves (1964) is credited with creating one of the more authoritative works in the field. So widespread has IGR become that it constitutes its own discipline, and most units of government have IGR sections or bureaus to deal with other governmental units.

Like federalism, IGR refers to the relations among various levels of

The Theoretical Context

government. Specifically, federalism concerns that form of government in which individual states recognize the partial, limited sovereignty of a central control while retaining residual power. As such, federalism is primarily concerned with national and state relations. More broadly construed, IGR is interested in the full array of governmental interactions: national-state, interstate, state-local, interlocal, national-state, and national-state-local. Unlike federalism, which tends to be concerned with top-down structural relations, from federal to state, IGR is concerned with the interaction between and among various levels. It presumes no superiority of any single link. Finally, IGR does not suffer the lexical—and conceptual—modifications associated with the prefixes to federalism: Creative Federalism, New Federalism, National Federalism, and Cooperative Federalism.

Several models of IGR have dominated the theoretical work. Advanced early on, the separated authority model suggests that boundaries between national and state governments are sharp and distinct. Local units are subsumed within the state units as creatures of the state, subject to creation, abolition, and the unfettered discretion of the state. In contrast, the inclusive authority model is premised on the belief that state and local governments depend on decisions that are nationwide in scope and arrived at by the national government or powerful economic interest, or by the intersection of the two. This approach places great weight on the federal government and less on local and state governments: "Nonnational institutions such as governors, state legislators, mayors, etc., have approached a condition of nearly total atrophy" (Wright 1978, p. 28). These two models, representing opposite ends of the spectrum, are joined by a third, intermediary approach. The overlapping authority model suggests that governmental operations involve national, local, and state units simultaneously. This approach assumes limited and dispersed ownership that is shared through a bargaining or exchange relationship. Moreover, it presumes limited jurisdictional autonomy. It is this model that dominates our intergovernmental system, and its prominence contributes to the ongoing need for service integration. Because structural relationships are perceived to be bargained and rebargained, the type and function of service integration structures are likely to be perpetually varied and changing.

This analysis of several theories of structure, though far from exhaustive, is illustrative of the variety that characterizes structuralist thinking. Structural theories attempt to explain and codify the relationships of suborganizational units to each other and to the whole. Those who examine area and function not only suggest that such structural differences are in part responsible for the ongoing organizational fragmentation but also attribute organizational resistance to change to the very structural characteristics that need to be altered. Moreover, such perspectives suggest that the press for fluctuating patterns of integration is inherent in the American system of intergovernmental relations. Local, state, and national levels of government are forced to recontour their relations with each piece of legislation, a reality that predicts continued fragmentation.

The Humanistic Perspective

In contrast to the structuralist perspective that regarded the organization as the defining element and subordinated individuals to it, early humanists injected human values and theories of individual development into the debate. Much of this orientation dates to the mid-1960s, but there are important antecedents earlier in the literature. For example, Barnard and other early human relations theorists believed that humans are "summoned to significance" by their participation in organizations (Barnard 1938). Humanists experiment with the notion of the organization as a social system that requires enlightened management. The hierarchical, noncollaborative modes that characterized the structuralists underemphasized the processes of coordination, decision making, and the role of human motivation in altering performance. The role of the executive, rather than to serve as the chief of command, is to maintain organizational communication, secure essential services from individuals, and formulate purposes and objectives. Comprising the technical components of leadership, these roles needed to be augmented by "creative morality," which inspired "ideality" and encouraged purposeful respect among all individuals in the organization. Such theories, while dramatically departing from structuralist precedent, still presumed that personal codes would coincide with the moral imperatives of the organization—which remained the primary unit of concern.

The Rise of the Individual

A turning point in the movement toward humanism could be regarded as the shift in primary emphasis from the organization to the individual. Maslow's thinking was instrumental in advancing this notion, in that he not only offered a perspective of human behavior that took motivation and need into account but saw that the needs of individuals are often at odds with those of institutions. Self-actualization, the apex of his hierarchy, was the inherent political right of individuals; correspondingly, institutions had the responsibility to support individuals in attaining that goal. Maslow even recommended a system of taxation, a moral accounting scheme, in which corporations would be rewarded according to the mental health of their employees:

> Some kind of tax penalty should be assessed against enterprises that undo the effects of a political democracy, of good schools, etc. and that make their people more paranoid, more hostile, more nasty, more malevolent, more destructive, etc. This is like sabotage against the whole society. And they should be made to pay for it. (Maslow 1965, pp. 59–60)

Setting the stage for countless derivations (Sloan 1964; Worthy 1950), this perspective was manifest notably in the work of McGregor (1960), who believed that Maslow's passion for individual rights could be married with the needs of the organization. McGregor's now renowned formulation of Theory X and Theory Y embodies this thinking. Theory X embraces the conventional notion that management consists of direction and control, which may be hard (coercion) or soft (permissive inducement). Theory Y portrays the role of management as creating conditions in which workers may control their activities in service to organizational goals. McGregor's contemporary, Argyris (1957), also grappled with the relationship of the individual to the institution, concluding that the inherent tensions of organizations were a result of the organizations' requirements for order and rationality rather than their malevolent intent to subjugate individual autonomy. Less optimistic, Bennis (1966) felt that the best one could hope to achieve was a satisfactory balance between the individual and the organization. Whatever the differences in perspective among these theorists, their humanistic orientations strongly influenced the emergence of the field of organizational development.

Organizational Democracy and Political Democracy

Fueled in part by the civil rights movement, the humanistic perspective became manifest in debates about organizational democracy, political power, and legitimacy. Bennis, for example, asserted that organizational democracy was the linchpin of a social system competing for survival in conditions of chronic change (Bennis 1966, p. 19). Like others espousing this orientation, Bennis called for employee participation, but the notions of organizational democracy were quite separate from political democracy. After all, he and his colleagues were concerned about human psychology and business management, not political science and public administration.

The applicability of these humanistic theories to public administration was a matter of interest, however. Conventionally, public administration held that politics and administration, like facts and values, were dichotomous terms. Nonetheless, with the growth of the humanist movement, as well as the complexities of increased specialization, more democratic, inclusive approaches to administration came to the fore. Such approaches emerged, in part, because there was mounting concern among political scientists that the organizations of government set up to protect the rights of individuals were in fact infringing upon, if not depleting them. Pluralist competition among interest groups served the rich (Lowi 1969), while institutions established to eradicate poverty perpetuated it (Piven and Cloward 1982). A new public administration movement of the late 1960s and early 1970s attempted to reconcile organizational and political considerations of democracy. But despite the best intentions of academics and many outside the academy, tension (perhaps healthy) existed between the goals of organizational democracy and the conventions of public administration.

In an effort to reconcile these perspectives for general purpose governments, Gardner (1976) noted the conventional theoretical dichotomy between policy and administration; but he also observes that the dichotomy between elected leaders setting policy and subordinate managers enacting or executing policy is largely a caricature, offering only a sense of the prevailing mode of "how things get done" (p. 15). Refuting such a simplistic conceptualization, Gardner suggests that the roles of leaders in the policy process are considerably more complex, tempered by value judgments and the recurring need for executives to bargain among power brokers and power constituencies. Acknowledging the special challenges faced by human service leaders, Gardner cited five categories of involvement for general purpose executives: "initial endorsement and effective delegation of leadership; sponsorship with staff monitoring of progress; policy leadership and management support to project staff; active managerial involvement; and personal political investments and formal management priority" (p. 20). Later, Gardner (1991b) suggested that elected officials can also serve as initiators of efforts to promote outcome accountability. Arguably, all of these categories could be depicted as transcending the conventional dichotomies associated with setting and enacting policy and management; they do not, however, violate the historic assumptions that support the humanistic approach to understanding service integration.

Leaders, Workers, and "Clients"

A vast literature on leadership theory would regard Gardner's (1976) tack as fitting squarely in the humanistic tradition, with a focus on the functional approach to leadership. Other approaches to understanding leadership have emerged, including the situational approach, which suggests that leaders fill roles and perform functions that are mediated by situational aspects of the environment. Another strand of research focuses on the traits of leaders—confidence, intelligence, ambition, perseverance, and sociability. Some investigators intertwine the two, suggesting that the performance of individual leaders is influenced not only by the personal traits of the leader but also by situational elements not in the leader's control. A third strand of work that emerged in the 1950s and 1960s examined the actual behaviors of leaders—authoritarian versus democratic, task-oriented versus social-emotional, employee-centered versus production-centered. More recent work, characteristic of cumulative approaches to theory building, suggests that leadership is a process of shared influences—functional, situational, traits, and behavioral.

Though much literature has focused on the leader as the primary agent of organizational change, the humanistic perspective of service integration accords a role to workers and clients or constituents as agents of reform. Functioning partially as an antidote to the cynicism, burnout, and alienation associated with classic bureaucracies, this approach is referred to as a bottom-up or worker-driven strategy for reform. Though such strategies are difficult to implement because practitioners are conventionally not legitimated by their organizations to function as agents of change, their value has become widely recognized (Resnick and Patti 1980). For example, the growing outcome-oriented literature indicates that when workers are engaged in planning and implementing change, their morale as well as personal and professional efficacy is quite high, and organizational outcomes or products are enhanced. This construct of organizational citizenship has taken root in business and industry and is now successfully finding its way into the human services and service integration efforts. It suggests that the primary approach to reform of the human services is through broad-based participation in efforts for change (Toch and Grant 1982).

Emanating from the civil rights era and the social movements from which it evolved and which it fueled, the human service field has come to recognize that change will not be appropriately conceived or durably sustained unless clients or constituents participate in it. One form of such engagement is taking place via family support programs and other programmatic attempts to involve families. But such programmatic engagement has been considered too benign. For example, Gilbert notes that "unless the base of concern for social change is broadened and those who claim to speak for the poor are formally accountable to the poor, the prospects are faint that citizen participation, regardless of its organizational sponsorship, will provide sufficient impulse for the democratization and reform of social welfare" (Gilbert 1970, p. 173).

The Systems Perspective

Building upon structuralist and humanistic perspectives, neither of which offered satisfactory explanations or models of organizational behavior independently, a third perspective—systems theory—developed. It appeared that structuralist approaches obscured the importance of human variables, whereas humanist expressions tended to relegate contextual variables to secondary or tertiary importance.

The origins of systems theory (so labeled) are often dated to Simon's *Administrative Behavior* (3d ed., 1976), first published in 1947, though actually the roots of this orientation go back to the functionalism of Bronislaw Malinowski and A. R. Radcliffe-Brown, which emphasized the interrelatedness of different aspects of social relationships and culture. The intellectual starting point for the functionalists was the social system conceived as a whole. Their perspective sought to understand and explain "the relationship of the parts to the whole in order to show how what appear to be isolated, if not inexplicable, social phenomena may fulfill some wider purpose related to the stability of society" (Silverman 1970, p. 5). At once the functionalists focused on the entirety of a system and were equally concerned with how systemic subunits (including subgroups of individuals) contributed to the stability and survival of the system as a whole. As a precursor to systems theory, functionalism was concerned with the efficiency and stability of the entire organism, not a single part. Moreover, it suggested that all organisms are forced to deal with change; change is regarded as an adaptation to externally imposed conditions that engender renewal.

Emanating from functionalist thinking, systems theory reflects the intellectual—though not operational—base of service integration. Systems theory suggests that each part of an organization can be understood only in its relation to other parts of the organization. Not only do the individual parts of the organization contribute to the whole, but so does the interrelatedness of the parts to one another. Organizations, conceived as wholes, have needs and goals that are superordinate to and conceptually separate from the needs and goals of individual members or parts. Further, echoing functionalist perspectives, organizational activity is understandable in terms of its relation to the external environment on which the organization depends for the realization of its purposes (Harmon and Mayer 1986, p. 158).

Intellectually, systems theory seems to be tightly aligned with the four service integration dimensions discussed in chapter 5. Client-centered service integration demands that coordination take place among those servicing the client and that such integration be constructed only when the subunits of service are clear. Program-centered service integration recognizes that various individual programs may contribute to the amelioration of a social problem, but that when they are amassed to coordinate or link services, such problems stand a better chance of being alleviated. Policy-centered service integration acknowledges that although policy initiatives have lives of their own and are total entities in and of themselves, they also exist within a broader context that shapes their formulation and implementation. And finally, organization-centered service integration shows that although subunits may have discrete goals, the consolidation of services under the umbrella of a superordinate and conceptually separate goal may be purposeful.

But systems theory, though the intellectual antecedent of service integration, has been regarded as an operational impediment, particularly as it was originally conceived and as it has been applied in the domain of public administration. It has been argued that systems theory, at least in its early embodiment, looked upon change as a threat to the survival of the system. First, change was considered as reflecting discontinuity (between systems) or disequilibrium (within the system). Hence, although it might be internally motivated, it was considered a sign of pathology rather than reaction to structural, demographic, or environmental factors. Second, systems theory places a premium on organizational survival. As such, change is instituted in the interest of restoring organizational equilibrium. If the change is successful and the system survives, equilibrium is restored; if it is unsuccessful and equilibrium is not restored, then the system is a failure, not meant to survive. It is a self-fulfilling prophecy that tends to reinforce the status quo and, with it, the existing power base.

Critics argue that the preoccupation with stability and order that emanated from this tradition has not adequately dealt with social conflict and the natural tensions that exist in and among organizations and between organizations and the communities they serve. This has led to the evolution of a body of work on open and closed systems theory and on organizational purposiveness (Gawthrop 1984) that has greater relevance for public administration. Gawthrop, for example, suggests that public organizations need to be designed and redesigned to deal with their changing environments. Public agency environments are porous, complex, and heterogeneous, requiring greater malleability and a value ethos that is willing to regard change not simply as a projection of the present but as a means of anticipating and altering present patterns. Moreover, such thinking has led scholars to consider the relationships among power, community control, and politics. Indeed, the functionalist approach needs to incorporate questions of distribution of power and its relationship to resource availability, as well as issues of conflict management and power politics (Coser and Larsen 1976).

Rather than accepting the constraints of systems theory, such work has encouraged a reconceptualization of systems theory from one of prediction and authoritative control to one of change and democratic control. Far more appropriate for public organizations, such a vision encourages greater attentiveness to issues of representation and inclusivity. Harmon and Mayer (1986) point out that in the process, general systems theory as a comprehensive framework for the *scientific* explanation of the social world has been tacitly abandoned in favor of the beginnings of a *social* philosophy as a new explanatory base. Such an approach is far more useful in the conceptualization and analysis of service integration and better reflects the spirit and philosophy of recent human service reformers.

Such theoretical orientations—structuralist, humanistic, and systems—need to be understood as somewhat co-linear, building upon and fueling one another, rather than as competing frameworks. The legacies of such theories—either individually or collectively—are manifest in the practice of service integration, the topic of the next part of this book.

Part III
Practical Realities: Implementing Service Integration

7

Action Frameworks

In Part II, we discussed definitional and theoretical approaches to service integration to try to make sense of an admittedly complex construct and to enable fairly rigorous explanations of the past. In many ways, the effort was retrospective sense-making. Helpful in that it explicated the conceptual antecedents of service integration, such theory-building, if it is to have utility, needs to find expression in practice.

But to date, the theoretical literature seems to have fallen short on this count. Its own proponents have charged that conceptualizations of integration are too global—that is, nondimensional—reflecting a prescriptive rather than an analytical perspective (Hagebak 1979; Martin, Chackerian, Imershein, and Frumkin 1983). Redburn (1977) contends that the construct lacks clarity regarding its substantive content and its multidimensional character, and Alford (1975) suggests that there is a conceptual confounding of service integration as an organizational innovation and as a quasi-political-ideological tool for change and social reform. Finally, it has been asserted that service integration, when it is applied to practice, confuses ends and means, never fully clarifying the causal connections between the two (Martin et al. 1983; Redburn 1977).

The purpose of this chapter is to examine some of the responses that have been offered to counter the charges of academic pie-in-the-skyism, detailing some of the important practical theories that have been propounded in hopes of illuminating possibilities for action or stimulating greater understanding of what has transpired. Indeed, there are a number of such praxis-based efforts, with many taking the form of explanatory frameworks. The discussion below focuses on those that appear most helpful in that, while varying by the phenomenon they try to explain, they stress the locus of linkages, the modes of or approaches to linkage, the activities associated with various linkage efforts, and the nature of temporal and causal relationships among linkages.

The Locus of Linkages

Several approaches have been taken to clarify the locus of integrative linkages, with attention to specific levels of government. Given the devolution of programmatic dollars and control to the states in the 1970s, a major focus was on linkages at the state agency level. Early in the service integration work there was some desire to better understand the differing roles that state agencies could pursue in the linkage process. To that end, a framework of linkage types was developed by the Council of State Governments (1974). This work suggests that there are differences among coordinated, consolidated, and integrated agencies. A coordinated agency is one in which formerly autonomous units retain most of their administrative and programmatic authority while a new agency is established to coordinate activities and programs. A consolidated agency is one in which most of the administrative and programmatic authority is transferred from previously autonomous agencies to a new agency, but operations are still conducted along program lines. Finally, an integrated agency is one in which all or most administrative authority is transferred to a new agency and, in addition, traditionally separate service patterns are intermeshed into a single program unit. Although helpful, these distinctions never came into common usage, in part because of state variability and in part because the more-common term "mega-agency" took hold.

Even if the terms had been popularized, this framework would not have been sufficiently robust because it did not give heed to the local role. In an effort to remedy this, recent work by Marzke, Chimerine, Morrill, and Marks (1992) has focused more clearly on service integration efforts in local settings. This work is helpful in that it further refines constructs of local collaboration, suggesting that there are four predominant types of local service integration efforts: (1) community-based multiservice centers, (2) targeted programs in community settings, (3) institution-based programs in community settings, and (4) school-based programs.

Community-based multiservice centers are sponsored by community-based organizations that are separate from the public delivery system. They maintain strong links with the community, a broad mission that is supported by a range of program offerings, open eligibility, and an unlimited duration of service. These efforts are linked via informal collaborative networks with other organizations that typically have case workers, program staff, and a wide array of funding sources.

Targeted programs in community settings are those that are more restricted in scope and address a targeted population. Typically, these services are available for limited times and maintain strong links to a particular government agency or program. They may be funded from private sources and/or a single public agency.

Institution-based programs in community settings are different from the above types in that they are usually sponsored by a consortium of public and private institutions and serve a broader population. They move beyond service delivery as the goal and attempt to alter systems.

Action Frameworks

They may be financed in part by redirected agency funds and may be administered by staff posted in allied agencies who frequently remain accountable to home agencies.

Finally, school-based programs, the fourth approach advanced by Marzke et al. (1992), are those that are typically located in schools and are supported by the school district. In this model, services are delivered in the schools, which retain much, though not all, programmatic and administrative authority.

These four approaches do not define the range of responses to the question of who links services, but they do reveal that an effort is under way to define more clearly the multiple loci for service integration efforts. Perhaps most noteworthy is the fact that none of these frameworks has undertaken to identify a comprehensive map of multiple loci in multiple levels. To date, frameworks of locus remain fragmented.

Modes of Linkage

Another issue that has plagued the field concerns how or by what modes linkages take place. Several helpful frameworks have been offered in an attempt to clarify this issue. Focusing on various approaches, Gans and Horton (1975) have identified three distinct modes by which service integration is accomplished: (1) voluntary coordination, (2) mediated coordination, and (3) directed coordination.

In voluntary coordination, the integrator (defined separately by HEW as "the organizational entity . . . responsible for coordinating the services of autonomous service providers through the development of interagency linkages" [1976, p. 9]) has dual responsibilities. It is responsible, first, for administering the provision of direct services and, second, for engaging others to ensure that the program is sufficiently comprehensive. An excellent example is Head Start, where directors are charged with responsibility for implementing the program and for linking families with additional services from community organizations.

In mediated coordination, the integrator is responsible primarily for developing linkages among autonomous service providers. In this

        Implementation

case, the integrator does not provide direct services. In early childhood services, this role is often assumed by resource and referral agencies who collate information on the services of various agencies and link parents with the services they need.

In directed coordination, "the integrator has the authority to mandate the development of linkages between legally subordinate providers" (Gans and Horton 1975, p. 50). Such an entity can compel action from division heads and engage parties, willing or not, in service integration.

Throughout their research, Gans and Horton (1975) found different effects for the different types. Voluntary coordination efforts were successful in reducing the duplication of work by service providers, but by far their greatest impact was to increase accessibility and continuity of services. Mediated coordination efforts had greater impact on community problem solving than did voluntary coordination efforts because they were able to use their resources to produce greater community accessibility and continuity of services. With no direct service responsibility, integrators were able to concentrate on the overall system and to support collaborative efforts that benefited multiple parties. Directed coordination was examined largely within the context of recent restructuring efforts which produced human resource agencies. At the time of the Gans and Horton study, these efforts were too fresh to be conclusively evaluated, but the authors felt that this approach held potential. In fact, they recommended that emphasis be placed on mediated and directed coordination efforts because these "pursue rationalization of the service delivery system on behalf of an entire class of clients rather than the manipulation of the delivery system for specific clients" (p. 22).

Another framework has been offered by O'Connor, Albrecht, Cohen, and Newquist-Carroll (1984). Predicated on work within youth services, this analysis suggests that there is a distinction between approaches that focus on changes in the service delivery system itself and those that focus on policy-making or administrative alterations. Moreover, they distinguish between those efforts that involve a fundamental redesign or reconceptualization and those that attempt to improve the performance of the existing components. Crossing these two dimensions, the authors arrive at four cells, each delineating an approach to service integration that closely parallels those of Agranoff and Pattakos (1979): government reorganization, policy management, service redesign, and program linkage.

Translating this framework into action, Agranoff (1991) suggests three public management activities that appear to be necessary for successful service integration: (1) the development of policies or strategies that support service integration at the services and program level; (2) the positioning of programs via the development of operating plans, so that case-level integration can be achieved; and (3) the development of local systems that interface multiple services. The first, policy or strategy development, takes many shapes; key among them is the interaction that must take place at the level of executive decisions—action by those who have the authority to shape the organization's domain. Stemming from these policies, organizational decisions should be handled by managers with a strong knowledge of their field and top-level authority from their respective organizations. Once these mechanisms are in place, service integration unfolds at the delivery level through the creation of various linkages. In contrast to the other modes of coordination, Agranoff (1991) is explicit in the linkages that must take place both within and among the tiers. Rather than separate, discrete approaches, Agranoff advocates an integrated approach to service integration.

Types of Linked Activities

By far the greatest amount of effort has been expended on the development of explanatory frameworks that address the myriad of specific activities being conducted under the rubric of service integration. It is perhaps in this domain where the development of frameworks has been the most advanced and the most helpful practically.

The writers of the seminal report of the Task Force on Administrative and Organizational Constraints to Services Integration (U.S. Department of Health, Education and Welfare 1972), though very concerned with the federal role in the movement, were careful to cast their analysis within a framework that delineated the activities of service integration into four kinds of program clusters: (1) managerial linkages, (2) operational linkages, (3) organizational linkages, and (4) physical linkages. Others who have followed have adapted this framework.

Managerial linkages refer to those efforts that enjoin planning, programming, budgeting, evaluation, and personnel components of two or more services. Such linkages can range from the development of a single source of authority for a particular component, to the establishment of similar techniques to carry out a task, to the sharing of information. Common managerial practices include sharing personnel and running joint training programs. Managerial linkages offer the spirit of collaboration while enabling agencies and professionals to maintain their autonomy. The task force pointed out that although these were necessary linkages, they were insufficient to meet the coordinative challenges facing HEW and society.

Operational linkages focus on the way services are delivered more than on the services themselves. They involve services that affect the client's entry into the service system (outreach and intake), decisions regarding the nature and amount of services the client will receive (diagnosis and referral), and the administrative efficacy of the system (information gathering, tracking, record keeping, and auditing). These linkages serve as the glue that binds services together and can help make a program far more effective. Because they are not threatening and can be implemented with some ease, they—like managerial linkages—are somewhat more common than other linkage strategies.

Organizational linkages refer to ties that are made between two agencies. Although the links vary from a common board to a common administrative body, in order for organizational linkages to be effective they must be accompanied by managerial or operational linkages. The organizational linkage model involves those linkage efforts that set up neutral agencies or bodies to oversee a service integration effort. This category was designed to include general purpose government as well as entities it might create.

Physical linkages are those designed to make services more accessible to clients. Collocation, one-stop shopping, and multiservice centers are examples of this form of linkage. Other less visible strategies may include organizing transportation to bring people and services together. Physical linkages do not need to be accompanied by managerial or operational linkages, but their chances for success are much greater if they are combined.

More concrete in orientation, other experts who examined service integration projects have noted different organizational clusters of linkage activities. Sampson, in an early work (1971), notes ten clusters, with the most frequently used program technique being coordinated planning. Such planning, like other strategies, appears in many guises—as councils, task forces, or within normal agency operations. The second most frequently identified activity was noncategorical program administration, followed by agreements to provide complementary services. Other coordinating mechanisms offered in the Sampson work include joint funding, target group advocacy, a leadership role for general purpose government, a shared management information system, shared core services, collocation of services, and mechanisms for follow-up and referral.

Dempsey (1982) specifies six categories of coordinating mechanisms: organizational realignment, inter-organizational decision making, ad hoc response to crisis, allocation of resources (budgeting), efforts to ensure information sharing between involved agencies, and efforts to enhance client convenience by improving service delivery.

A particularly helpful framework, introduced in chapter 5, distinguishes between efforts directed toward systemic changes, loosely identified as administrative/management strategies, and those directed at improving direct services. For example, using this approach, Kahn and Kamerman (1992) have compiled an excellent framework, with the following falling into the administrative/management category: interagency agreements; interagency councils or committees; collocation of services; single point of intake/assessment; flexible, pooled, or decategorized funding; coapplication procedures; coordination or consolidation of programs, budgeting, planning, and administration; involvement of a lead agency; and comprehensive management information systems. In contrast, case-oriented strategies include case management; case conferences or case review panels; individualized child or family case assessment and service plan development; case monitoring or outcome monitoring; regard of the family as the treatment or service unit; home visits; and flexible funds or resources at the disposal of the frontline worker.

Perhaps the most comprehensive framework of linkage strategies was conceived by the Research Group et al. (1972b) and Gans and Horton (1975). The framework was predicated on the assumption that different configurations of project characteristics have different impacts on the accessibility, continuity, and efficiency of service delivery, and that these configurations result in the development of different integrating linkages. Predicting the Kahn and Kamerman framework (1992) mentioned above, the typology broke all linkage mechanisms into administrative linkages and direct service linkages.

The administrative linkage category was subdivided into four categories; fiscal, personnel practices, planning and programming, and administrative support services. Each of these categories was quite broad, comprising a variety of mechanisms germane to that category. The fiscal category included joint budgeting, joint funding, fund transfer, and purchase of service. Personnel practices included consolidated personnel administration, joint use of staff, staff transfer, staff outstationing, and collocation. Planning and programming included joint planning, joint development of operating policies, joint programming, information sharing, and joint evaluations. Administrative support services included record keeping, grants management, and support services. The direct service linkage category was divided into two: core services and modes of case coordination. Core services included outreach, intake, diagnosis, referral, and follow-up. Modes of case coordination included case conference, case coordinator, and core team.

The development of this linkage approach enabled the authors to delve fully into the processes and outcomes of service integration, and to make correlations between the mode of coordination and the linkage strategies used. For example, the researchers noted a correlation between the use of direct service linkages and voluntary projects. In contrast, there were distinct correlations between the use of administrative linkages and mediated and directed projects. This framework helped investigators realize that what had been previously conceived as independent linkage strategies were indeed interrelated. Though no single linkage strategy inevitably led to any other single strategy, clusters of efforts were discernible.

The Nature of Temporal and Causal Relationships

The conceptual literature on service integration is studded with efforts to understand the causal and temporal relationship between client-based services and administrative-based services. Can one be fully successful without the other? If not, what is the necessary sequencing of these strategies?

Martin et al. (1983) report on Lynn's 1980 conception of an ideally integrated service delivery system. Lynn identifies five distinct dimensions of service integration: a unified administrative structure, local administrative control, coordinative case management, collocation of multiple program services, and a single point intake/application procedure. Each dimension of this schema implies different outcomes at different levels of the system. For example, collocation may have the greatest benefit for clients with little impact on administration. On the other hand, a unified administrative structure would have more direct and immediate implications for executive staff in the integration effort itself, with limited immediate effect on direct line workers, and perhaps no direct influence on clients. Combining structural (administrative unification), procedural (single intake), and geographic (collocation) factors, this framework seems to presume that though such strategies have synergy, they do not all need to happen concurrently. Good case management can exist, for example, in the absence of a unified administrative structure.

To clarify the associations among these strategies, Martin et al. (1983) have offered a powerful and sophisticated framework that helps explain the nature of causality among factors. Essentially, they posit two models, one where exogenous forces (such as unified administrative structure and local administrative control) precede and determine the development and trajectory of endogenous factors (like coordinative case management, collocation, single intake process, and efficiency in resource utilization) that depend on and exist within those that are exogenous. In the alternative model, the endogenous factors listed above are regarded as exogenous, not necessarily dependent on the existence of a unified administrative structure to institute and maintain case management, collocation, and so forth. The core question addressed by this conception is whether various activities can function independently or whether they depend on others for the successful realization of outcomes. Some argue that only when the unified structure exists can integrative mechanisms (collocation, case management, etc.) produce their intended benefits for clients (Morris and Lescohier 1978). Others (including Martin et al. 1983) suggest that in the absence of a unified structure—which is so often the case—integrative mechanisms can be beneficial and produce positive outcomes for clients, particularly if there are alternative arrangements for ensuring adherence to common goals (such as interagency agreements).

In working though the issues of relationality and causality, Martin et al. (1983) also help distinguish between the effects of linkage efforts and the efforts themselves. They note that greater linkages among providers are a "result of integration, not a part of it" (p. 759). Clearly, linkages can occur without integration—that is, linkage activities can be established in the absence of a unified administrative structure. But to sustain such linkages, integrative mechanisms are necessary.

Though less than perfect, the literature on frameworks is helpful in chronicling the locus, the modes, and the nature of the efforts undertaken in the name of service integration. Having addressed various conceptual approaches to understanding service integration, we now turn to the practical barriers that face the implementation of integration efforts.

8

Barriers and Incentives

Mother Teresa, who won the Nobel Peace Prize for her
work with the poor and dying in Calcutta's slums, was
once asked by Senator Mark Hatfield, "Don't you get
awfully discouraged when you see the magnitude of the
poverty and realize how little you can really do?"—to
which she replied: "God has not called me to be
successful, he has called me to be faithful."
—Paul Theroux (1981)

The devotees of service integration bear a strong
resemblance to Mother Teresa, for despite tireless efforts and what appear to be unbeatable odds, they remain persistently faithful. The challenges to both are
enormous, the barriers to their success ubiquitous.

One of the primary reasons for the research and
practice agenda of the 1970s was to gain practical

lessons in implementation that could help in shaping future legislation and practice. Perhaps the jewel of this literature regards information on barriers. Indeed, in conducting a comprehensive review, Yessian (1991) notes, "We find that the clearest lessons learned are about the factors that inhibit services integration" (p. 6).

Early discussions of barriers painted a bleak picture. Gans and Horton (1975) concluded that field conditions were generally "hostile to service integration efforts" (p. 84). Other studies of efforts to link comprehensive service programs found the constraints so "formidable that only under exceptional conditions could localities develop and maintain [the] programs" (Weatherly et al. 1987, pp. 79–80).

This chapter explores specific barriers and incentives to service integration recounted from the perspectives of researchers, practitioners, and policymakers who have been engaged in this approach to reform. Two caveats should be noted, however. First, the nomenclature for barriers is confusing. Some use the term *barriers*, while others use *inhibitors* or *weaknesses* (Sampson 1971). This discussion addresses all three factors—barriers, inhibitors, weaknesses—that delay or prevent the implementation of service integration.

The second caveat concerns the lack of a standard scheme for classifying the barriers. Some schemata focus on inputs and some on outputs; some (typically earlier schemata) stress organizational factors and others (typically later schemata) focus more broadly on sociopolitical and contextual factors. Consequently, an interesting paradox emerges. As the service integration strategies themselves became more specialized or more targeted, the factors that accounted for their implementation' successes or failures became more broadly construed. In retrospect, the literature seems to suggest that initially we were attempting to understand the whole cosmos through the eye of a needle; later, recognizing the dilemma, we magnified the needle's eye to look at more narrowly delimited domains. Such refinements suggest both the complexity of the challenge and the crudeness of our knowledge as we embarked on a national service integration strategy in the 1970s. Nonetheless, many of the basic barriers have been clearly elucidated since that time.

The Basic Barriers

In the early 1970s the Task Force on Administrative and Organizational Constraints was asked to examine "the administrative and organizational practices which impede the integration of services" (U.S. Department of Health, Education and Welfare 1972, p. 1). The group was also charged with making recommendations that HEW could enact to overcome such barriers. Noting the difficulties, the report of the task force offers the following disclaimer: "It will become quickly apparent to the reader that the original goals of the Task Force were only partially achieved. The way has nevertheless been cleared for a more concerted and intelligent effort. . . . The corner known as 'institutional reform' has been turned" (p. 2). Despite the disclaimer, and perhaps framed by its charge, the task force's analysis notes four categories of barriers: attitudes, the size and complexity of the system, the locus and authority of responsibility, and departmental organization, procedures, and regulations. Since publication of the report, each of these categories has been affirmed in the literature, and additional concerns have been delineated.

The 1972 report noted that the most persistent factor that impeded service integration was attitudes, both of individuals and of organizations. Acknowledging that such attitudes are the cause and the effect of the organizational system in which bureaucrats work, the report attributed attitudinal barriers to many kinds of factors: historical, legislative, and educational. It noted that HEW was organized along professional lines, with services divided into separate and largely autonomous program units. Because staff identified more with their own units than with their professions, and because responsibilities and rewards reflected this pattern, the incentives for collaboration were limited. Strongly reinforced throughout the intergovernmental system, the pattern did not break down even when there was recognition of the interconnectedness of individuals' needs for service. Though there had been attempts to use "human services generalists," whose job it was to cut across program and departmental lines, these efforts had been scattered and their impact sparse. Such lack of success had been attributed to the fact that generalists encountered tremendous resistance from specialists. The report also stated that while professional values may be important inhibiting factors, so too are attitudes toward the government and toward government programs. This analysis noted deep skepticism on the part of local service providers regarding the depth of HEW's commitment to service integration: "They have scant experiential evidence, at best, on which to base a faith that DHEW officials mean it when they utter the services integration rhetoric" (U.S. Department of Health, Education and Welfare 1972, p. 17).

The second inhibiting factor noted in the 1972 report was the size and complexity of the system. Local service providers were overwhelmed by "the number of doors to open, the professional keys necessary to open them, the mazes of paperwork . . . the length of time between the conception of an idea and fulfillment, the budgetary uncertainties" (p. 17). Stated more bureaucratically, the regulatory and processing procedures, coupled with varying eligibility and reporting requirements, were recognized as burdensome. Such demands had serious operational consequences for local providers, who had to keep up with request-for-proposal announcements and their unending requirements, and with shifting priorities—an unbearable burden for those trying to meld programs. Such a context forces competition for scarce resources among those who should be collaborating to distribute them fairly and rationally.

Diffuse locus of authority and responsibility, in particular a lack of role clarity, was cited as the third barrier. Locals did not know where in the federal morass the service integration initiatives resided, and who the advance people were. Moreover, they perceived a lack of support and little local leadership. Service integration seemed to be lost in the bureaucratic cracks from top to bottom, and this condition was subsequently used as the rationale to reinforce the role of general purpose governments in integration efforts.

Finally, the report underscored the "contempt for excessive program requirements and narrow guidelines" (p. 18) expressed by local service providers. While acknowledging the reality of many such inconsistencies and burdens, the report also noted that some of the regulatory barriers were nonexistent or interpreted incorrectly. Clearly the adamancy of local concern left its mark, as the report chronicled within-department dilemmas: the categorical nature of HEW funding and the variation in program decentralization that forced local program directors to deal with both the regional and the federal levels. Furthermore, the report listed three additional problems: the lack of background information to locals regarding service integration, the lack of technical assistance (and the nature of that assistance which did exist), and the lack of authority of the regional directors (and correspondingly the lack of authority of their staffs for service integration efforts).

In sum, the report noted that such findings hindered not only project-by-project funding but also a more responsive and efficient federal system in general. It said that, on the one hand, localities and states had little incentive to get ahead of the action while, on the other hand, the national system could never be sure that it was using its dollars effectively or equitably. Given these findings, the report suggested that the outlines for federal reform were beginning to emerge. Presumably such a system would place more responsibility with general purpose governments while fortifying technical assistance capacities and streamlining regulation at the federal level.

Philosophic Barriers

The basic barriers discussed above are deeply entrenched in service approaches and in the attitudes and philosophies that shroud the system and envelop workers and clients. Blum (1982), for example, discusses the dilemmas associated with programmatic and funding fragmentation and with organizational structure, underscoring the government's role in hastening service fragmentation and noting that "the organizational and financial barriers to service coordination can be intimated merely by listing the major government health and social services programs" (p. 79). As a specific example, Blum cites the case of institutional and residential care. There had been a propensity, rooted in traditional beliefs, to sequester those unable to care for themselves. Hence the retarded, the aged, and the handicapped were cared for in institutions that were self-contained, isolated communities. Until the deinstitutionalization movement and the stipulation of a least-restrictive environment for special education—both attempts to integrate services—philosophic predispositions inhibited effective collaboration of mainstream and nonmainstream populations.

Others raise similar concerns. Firestone and Drews (1987), for example, note that such philosophic barriers extend even to questions of which clients should be served and what services should be rendered. They note that different professionals view such questions differently, so that "typically educators have a narrower view of clientele and services than mental health professionals" (p. 3). Ideas about collaboration also vary when professional views do not incorporate any explicit philosophical commitment to linkage.

Fiscal and Human Resource Barriers

Like others before them, Firestone and Drews also discuss limited human and fiscal resources as critical inhibitors to service integration. Speaking about fiscal resources, they note that limited service capacity contributes to fundamental tensions regarding resource allocations. Moreover, when service integrationists seek dollars for their own programs, they are often perceived as doing so at the expense of direct service programs, evoking further alienation between service practitioners and service integration advocates. Competition for scarce resources is routinely cited as a barrier to service integration (Weatherley et al. 1987).

Beyond the tensions created by competition for scarce extant resources, Yessian (1991) notes that the lack of additional direct and consistent dollars for service integration has been one of the six barriers to implementation. Additional funds, not always forthcoming, have often been vital to establishing service integration mechanisms such as collocated services, case management, and client information systems. Without them, the necessary infrastructure to support service integration often cannot be built. Though badly needed, such resources are difficult to acquire because they are seen by legislators and agency administrators as the means to open the well. Not generally regarded as investments, dollars spent on service integration are regarded as money down the drain because not only are they costly in and of themselves, but they often precipitate calls for more dollars for themselves or for direct services.

It should be noted, however, that the absence of resources is not always an inhibitor to service integration. In some cases, the lack of funds actually fosters the need for and pursuit of service integration. Nonetheless, it is clear that once established, service integration efforts are accelerated by the presence of fiscal resources.

Similarly, the lack of expert human resources has also been regarded as a significant barrier to implementing service integration efforts. Dollars are needed to recruit and maintain qualified staff, a barrier cited frequently in Kusserow's (1991) analysis of service integration for children and families in crisis. Firestone and Drews (1987) extend the range of human barriers to include those associated with the need for individuals who have the requisite qualities to implement service integration. Weatherley et al. (1987) differentiate between general leadership, grantsmanship, political leadership, institutional leadership, and administrative leadership. From their work on comprehensive services for pregnant and parenting adolescents, they note that barriers to success can include a rapid turnover of leaders and a lack of leaders who come from the community. Lack of political support for such efforts is a barrier, as is the lack of community supports from social service agencies, the United Way, and the schools. The need for effective leadership and its absence has been cited as a barrier by others (Gans and Horton 1975), though many are quick to note that such leadership is not necessarily tied to a specific professional credential.

Incorporated within the human resources barrier is the lack of a suitable capacity to train prospective leaders and workers in service integration. Successful integration efforts demand a cross-disciplinary, holistic perspective on human, child, and family needs and development—a perspective not usually afforded by the current, categorically oriented training apparatus. Further, service integration requires negotiation and creative problem-solving skills, as well as the ability to apply fresh concepts to entrenched traditions. The inability of the current training system to provide individuals with these skills and perspectives—compounded by its continued focus on narrowly delimited professional fields—poses a serious barrier to implementing successful service integration.

Political Barriers and the Nature of Change

Another set of barriers relates to the conflict between an institution's desire to preserve its own mission and its need to accommodate change. Inducted into service integration to meet an organizational mission, individuals are often reluctant to accept the new mission; this is perhaps why so many of the service integration efforts have been presented as "can-do" strategies rather than "rethink" philosophies. When presented as practical tasks, they are easier to incorporate into individual philosophies and into organizational cultures. Nevertheless, philosophical support for service integration can be quite marginal.

Lynn (1980) notes that organizational change is essentially a political issue (p. 174), explaining that change strategies need powerful constituencies—a lack that is mentioned frequently in the service integration literature. Though human services have traditionally had strong constituencies, they exist for specific target groups—the handicapped, the aged—and for targeted programs for these groups. Coalescing advocates beyond their turf and inspiring them to action for what may be perceived as a threatening or even counterproductive effort has been problematic. The result has been that service integration rarely has had a practitioner constituency. Affirming this perspective, Yessian (1991) notes that "those supporting SI efforts tend to be diffused and with rare exception less forceful in their advocacy" (p. 7).

Indeed, part of the problem is that analysts and implementors tend to regard service integration as a technical activity, largely because it is technically complex. Such an orientation, however, sweeps from view (1) the limitations of a technical strategy in solving a systemic problem and (2) the need to identify and mobilize powerful constituencies outside the service community. Weatherley et al. (1987) discuss this; Lynn (1980) makes it explicit, exhorting advocates of such changes to consider gubernatorial, legislative, and combined executive-legislative strategies, and noting that the challenge is not easy because state officials tend to have a far greater sense of responsibility to economy and efficiency in government operations than toward the effectiveness of coverage in the human services.

Technical Barriers

However important the political barriers, understanding the technical barriers to service integration is critical as well. Sampson (1971) notes that many of the early efforts by HEW were slow to start up, with considerable time required for the beginning phases of the efforts. Such slowness of start-up is not necessarily a barrier, for many comprehensive initiatives do take time to launch. Lacking momentum at the outset, however, may reflect other missing ingredients that are not only start-up but implementation barriers—namely, lack of personnel, political support, and technical staff competence. Sampson observes that many of the projects she investigated did lack the staff qualified to complete the tasks at hand. In particular, many of the efforts drew on the expertise of individuals trained to consider problems and delivery of services according to specific categorical guidelines and regulations. Equally important, Sampson points out that many of the projects had only the most general objectives, too vague to be quantified as outcomes. Frequently, alterations in process, rather than alterations in outcome, were proxy objectives. Finally, while dependent on information as their stock-in-trade, many of the projects lacked the capacity to collect, analyze, or utilize data effectively.

The implementation of comprehensive data systems is so important to service integration and so complicated a task as to warrant special discussion. Data systems occasion mistrust because people find them impersonal and at the same time believe that the risk that confidential personal information will be misused is great. Of particular sensitivity are data systems that monitor or require adherence to procedural rules and those that give organizational visibility to workers' activities (Cotter 1981). Indeed, the barriers have been so strong that they have been analyzed, and a continuum of acceptance/resistance levels for both the provision of data and the use of system information—ranging from enthusiastic support to deliberate sabotage—has been developed (London 1976).

A third technical barrier to effective coordination is the apparent inability to coordinate financing mechanisms. Farrow and Joe (1992) suggest three reasons for this. First, the inherent nature of categorical funding, with its narrow access criteria and problem-focused orientation, limits creative and permissive uses of funding. Fairly, the authors note that such categorization is fortified by an "iron triangle" of "specialized funding, specialized professional purviews, and specialized agency organization" (p. 61). The second difficulty in using funds effectively is the crisis orientation that is triggered by child and family need. Funds are routinely available in response to an identified need, but not as a mechanism to prevent problems. Finally, Farrow and Joe suggest that the lack of a universal entitlement approach forces the "screening out" of families and reinforces a narrow approach to service delivery.

One partial solution, as we have seen, has been to grant authority to local and state governments for human service integration. Although generally applauded, this remains an imperfect strategy in that there is a fundamental mismatch in the control of resources, with the federal government dominating state and local spending in the human services and the states controlling education resources. The human services budget is massive, outstripping other domestic expenditures, and by setting rules that govern program design, operation, and federal reimbursement claims, federal control is further extended. But perhaps even more significant than the flow of dollars, states and localities are often used as surrogates for federal intent in the social services. Indeed, the federal government has—until quite recently—dominated most discussions regarding the intent and direction of human services (Copeland and Iversen 1981).

Inevitably, with federal dominance comes fragmentation. There is no congressional requirement that new programs dovetail with existing ones; to the contrary, the politics that gave rise to the program might work against such fiscal coordination. For example, different pieces of legislation have different funding pathways associated with them, including flow from the federal to a single state agency, flow from federal to allied agencies, flow from federal to local agencies (as in Head Start), and flow from federal agencies to a client. Such design differences are impediments to coordination. Funding factors emanating from these different design conditions—reimbursement strategies, audit requirements, client eligibility—further compound fiscal fragmentation.

Codifying the Barriers

Given their abundance, it is not surprising that efforts to codify the range of barriers fill the literature. Firestone and Drews (1987) divide them into two primary categories: those that deal with interagency conflict and those that impede direct services. Interagency conflict includes the barriers that impede the interaction of agencies with some regularity, ranging from minor incidents to permanent blockages to relations. Service blockages are those that prevent services from being linked, keeping clients from receiving the kinds and amount of services needed. Firestone and Drews indicate that these may appear to be independent, with interagency conflict not necessarily blocking service delivery or service blockages not necessarily occurring where there is agency conflict. They do acknowledge, however, that certain types of barriers—regulatory, for example—can contribute to both barrier sets.

Perhaps the most thorough analysis of barriers has been done by the Research Group and Kaplan, Gans, and Kahn (1972b; see also Gans and Horton 1975). The work is conceptually significant because it highlights the context for service integration efforts—a construct that, because it was buried in other analyses, had not been clearly articulated. Note that in their discussion of barriers, context is offered as the first consideration: "Services integration is less likely to occur even given the already unreceptive environment in which services integration must take place" (Gans and Horton 1975, p. 6).

The typology they offer delineates eight major categories of inhibitors: (1) integrator's (either individual or group) objectives and attitudes; (2) service provider's objectives and attitudes; (3) grant administration policies and procedures; (4) project structure and operations; (5) environmental influences; (6) project staff; (7) technical and logistical factors; and (8) service provider's policies and procedures. These categories are presented in order of the frequency with which they were cited by practitioners engaged in service integration projects. That no single category was an important inhibitor in more than 20 percent of the cases reflects the diversity of factors that affect service integration and the degree to which they vary by site, project intention, and context.

The findings on the integrator's objectives and attitudes are important because it was noted that when the integrator is focused on its own direct service delivery, attention to integration of services may be curtailed. It may be hard for an individual or an agency to be both the deliverer of services and the coordinator of them across agencies. In part, this is due to the immediate demands of direct service delivery in contrast to the less-than-immediate press for service integration efforts. Service delivery is the squeaky wheel that gets the grease. Closely aligned with the first barrier, the second—service provider objectives and attitudes—is the desire of service providers to retain prerogatives with respect to the control of service delivery. A clear barrier to service integration is the unwillingness of providers to relinquish control, especially to super- or mega-agencies.

Structural factors account for the next two categories of barriers. The categorical grant system inhibited service integration through prohibitions against joint funding, fund transfers, and the commingling of dollars. The research also noted that demonstration grants—in addition to categoricals—were in some respects inhibitors to service integration, in that they were often too short and too "special" to fit in with mainstream integration efforts. Implementation was also exacerbated by conflicting guidelines or information from regional and federal offices. Even information from the same HEW office was often noted as being contradictory. Project structure was a barrier in that often the leaders did not include staff in planning; poor administration, unclear role delineation, and insufficient supervision were also cited.

Environmental influences were mentioned as being among the most significant barriers, with the actions and attitudes of the funding source ranking high among them. Local and state government opposition to changes in the service delivery system inhibited the integration efforts considerably.

Finally, conflicts between the staff of the integrator agency and the staff of the service delivery agency frequently occurred when the integrator agency staff proposed changes in procedures and deviated from bureaucratic routine. Technical and service provider inhibitors focused around the lack of effective communication systems, particularly in efforts where there was no separate linkage staff.

Facilitators of Service Integration

This chapter has emphasized barriers, largely because the literature reflects this bias. Suffering from a deficit orientation, service integration is typically regarded as unsuccessful, cited for what it cannot do rather than for its accomplishments. Accordingly, much research is directed at explaining the failures.

When the research has focused on facilitators of service integration, much of what is discussed simply reverses the barriers. For example, a review of Gans and Horton (1975) reveals that six of the eight facilitating factors are also listed as barriers (environmental influences, service provider objectives and attitudes, grant administration policies and procedures, project structure and operations, project staff, and technical and logistical features). Two barriers were eliminated: integrator objectives and priorities, and service provider policies and procedures; two facilitating factors were added in their stead: role of the director or board and incentives for participation. Support from the environment was cited as the first and strongest facilitator. (It was the fifth barrier.) Cited as components of this facilitation were support from the external sociopolitical environment and the cooperative environment created by direct actors in the project.

The role of the director or board is a critical factor that facilitated success when the director or board had formal authority over the total project. In addition to their authority and their political-administrative contacts, the personalities of the director and the assistant director were regarded as important accelerators. Incentives for participation were also considered important, particularly if the service providers received some financial benefit, if the integrator functioned as a mediator or buffer in overcoming problems with other agencies, and if the linkages were developed at the suggestion of a prestigious external source.

In sum, the barriers to service integration are anchored in the system it is trying to reform. In many ways they are its raison d'être. Yet it is also clear from the literature that barriers are not experienced the same way in all contexts—that settings vary and that, though the presumption of universal problems may be correct, the assumption of universal barriers is probably not.

9
Strategies

Despite the numerous and extensive barriers to service integration described in chapter 8, reformers have succeeded in developing effective strategies, implemented individually or as elements of a coordinated plan, to bring down the barriers and capitalize on incentives to integration. For purposes of clarity, the analysis in this chapter is divided into the domains outlined by Agranoff and Pattakos (1979) and detailed in chapter 5: (1) service delivery, (2) program linkages, (3) policy management, and (4) organizational structure; renamed herein as (1) client-centered integration, (2) program-centered integration, (3) policy-centered integration, and (4) organizationally centered integration, respectively. It should be noted that occasionally a strategy is used to fulfill functions in more than one domain. Such cases have been described in the section that is most proximal to their intent.

Client-Centered Integration

Focusing on the point of interaction between service providers and consumers, client-centered integration works within the fragmented delivery system to link individuals with needed services from disparate programs.

Case Management

The primary method of achieving such linkages is case management, a process in which an individual or unit is assigned to assist a client (individual or family) in developing and executing a coordinated plan of services. Not restricted to a specific service, case managers are able to gain a deeper understanding and make a more holistic assessment of client needs, establish a stronger, more productive relationship with the client, and serve as a single locus of responsibility for meeting client needs throughout the process of service delivery (Gans and Horton 1975).

Case management has been described in the literature as "the bridge between the interests of the categorical service providers and the complex needs of the 'whole' client" (Agranoff and Pattakos 1979, p. 33); "a set of logical steps and a process of interaction within a service network which assure that a client receives (an array of) needed services in a supportive, effective, efficient, and cost-effective manner" (Weil and Karls 1992; qtd. Family Impact Seminar 1992, p. 4); and, in the 1981 Omnibus Budget Reconciliation Act, "a system under which responsibility for locating, coordinating, and monitoring a group of services rests with a defined person or group" (Section 2176; qtd. Family Impact Seminar 1992, p. 5). Breaking down specific functions of case management, Agranoff (1977) includes (1) assessment of client need, (2) development of a cross-program service plan, (3) arrangement for service delivery, (4) service monitoring and assessment, and (5) evaluation and follow-up.

Investigating Definitional Ambiguity

Beyond these conceptual principles and outlines, however, case management in practice remains a somewhat malleable strategy, showing great variety in its focus and goals. Definitions of case management tend to be as varied and elusive as they are of service integration. Indeed, case management has been likened to "a Rorschach test. An individual, an agency, or a community will project onto case management its own particular solution to the problems it faces" (Schwartz, Goldman, and Churgin 1982, p. 1006).

One explanation for the range of shapes case management can assume is its dependence on context, and on the variations in context that occur over time. Not a specific, isolable event, case management is an ongoing, fluctuating process, responsive to changes in the needs of clients (Stein 1981) as well as to other factors, including the nature of the service system that the case management system is both supported by and designed to address (Intagliata 1981; National Conference on Social Welfare 1981; Ross 1980). The result of this context dependency is a conception of case management that varies *within an individual case* as needs are met and new needs arise, *within a service delivery system* as higher systemic reforms are effected, and *across systems* with different structures, resources, and relationships among programs.

Further contributing to definitional ambiguity, the Family Impact Seminar (1992) suggests that there are two separate rationales for case management—that it owes allegiance to two separate entities: the system and the client. Though the basic activity of linking clients with services remains constant in each case, the system-centered rationale is primarily concerned with program accountability and cost effectiveness, while the client-centered rationale focuses on issues of accessibility and quality of service. Depending on their focus, different integration efforts may emphasize one allegiance over the other, with direct implications for the goals and processes of their case management systems.

An effect of emphasizing one of these two rationales over the other is on the degree to which case management either involves and empowers individuals receiving services or subjects them to the will of the system. At one extreme, the process of case management may be controlled entirely by the case manager, who alone determines clients' needs and devises service plans without client input. Indeed, some have suggested that such a system of management is implied in the term itself, labeling it "system-centric and paternalistic" (Family Impact Seminar 1992, p. 4) for suggesting that human beings need to be "managed." Further, Skarnulis (1981) notes the "potential for depersonalization, dehumanization, and social distance between server and served" (p. 25) created by using the word *case* rather than *human being*.

At the other end of the spectrum, client–case manager equity is stressed, and clients are involved in all stages of the process—in determining their needs, creating service plans, and deciding when services are no longer needed. One method of ensuring such client input is the use of written contracts between the client, the case manager, and service providers, delineating the responsibilities and expectations of all parties (Agranoff and Pattakos 1979; Stein 1981). In order to evaluate programs according to their involvement and empowerment of clients, Gerry (in press) has devised an assessment tool that asks such questions as who determines what services are needed; who sets service goals and priorities; is jargon used, and who understands it; who schedules services; and who determines if services are provided effectively.

Approaches to Case Management

Though case management is based on providing a consolidated point of client contact within a fragmented system, the responsibility for management may be assigned in a variety of ways. Most sources outline at least two approaches to case management: via the individual, often a generalist who takes full responsibility for providing core management services from intake to termination, and via an interdisciplinary team, composed usually of specialists who together assess client need and plan a service strategy, often with one team member playing a team leadership/client-service liaison role (Family Impact Seminar 1992; Gans and Horton 1975; Intagliata 1981; Stein 1981).

In addition, numerous intermediate approaches have been noted. In the "sequential" approach, the responsibility for creating linkages shifts as the client progresses through the stages of service delivery; for example, different staff members may be involved when the client moves from diagnosis to referral. The "coordination" approach allows for an alternate method in which responsibility is divided not by sequence but according to the needs of individual family members; frequently used in child welfare, this approach may assign one worker to the parents and another to a child in out-of-home care (Stein, Gambrille, and Wiltse 1977). Gans and Horton (1975) suggest as their intermediate approach the use of "case conferences"; different from team management in its involvement of external service providers and ad hoc status, this approach is often used in conjunction with an individual case manager who convenes conferences as needed.

Experimentation over the past twenty years has not proven the superiority of any one approach, but interesting advantages and disadvantages of each have been noted. The sharing of responsibility found in coordinated and team case management has been found to facilitate greater risk taking (Stein 1981) and may provide a greater likelihood of continuous availability of assistance to the client and help to reduce staff burnout (Test 1979). Teams, however, have poor longevity owing to staff turnover (Stein 1981) and require greater ongoing effort and organization (Gans and Horton 1975). In addition, a study of SITO projects raised the question of whether the higher costs associated with team management (in comparison with individual case management) were warranted in the light of its benefits (John 1977, cited in Stein 1981). At the other end of the continuum, individual case managers provide continuity both across services and throughout the service delivery process. Further, reflecting the holistic approach of integrated service delivery, assigning case management to a generalist rather than a specialist allows specialist service providers to focus on the problems for which they were trained and to "rest assured that [the client's broader social needs] are being taken care of within the larger system" (Bourne 1974, p. 668, qtd. Agranoff and Pattakos 1979, p. 36).

Program-Centered Integration

Program-centered integration strategies may range from informal, limited agreements among programs to more formal, extensive, and ongoing linkages, and include collocation, developing shared information systems, sharing staff, joint programming and planning, and fiscal linkages.

Collocation

Collocation attempts to coordinate programs by eliminating the geographic fragmentation of service providers, uniting them within a single, all-purpose facility. The proposed benefits of collocation are many, though the actual effects often fall short of expectations if collocation is not implemented in conjunction with other linkage strategies.

Bringing service providers together under one roof has been lauded as increasing both program visibility and client accessibility to services by minimizing scheduling and transportation barriers (Austin 1982; Gans and Horton 1975). Collocation may further enhance accessibility by concentrating services in areas with high populations of clients in need (National Academy of Public Administration 1977). Overhead and administrative costs may be saved by sharing space, administrative support, and office equipment, and staff travel and communication costs may be reduced. Collocation has also been praised as a pathway to improved communication and more appropriate and immediate client referrals among programs, thereby establishing a more holistic approach to service delivery.

Despite these lofty claims, the literature repeatedly stresses that collocation in and of itself is incapable of achieving much more than what its name implies—co-location—and that integration reform at the administrative level is a critical ingredient in realizing the above benefits. Though other program-centered linkages are often conducted at collocated centers, the degree of linkage that actually occurs is a result not simply of collocation but of "the willingness of the participants to change their normal way of operation" (Agranoff and Pattakos 1979, p. 54). Mudd (1982) states the point succinctly: "Walls that insulate bureaucracies from each other are organizational, not physical" (p. 29). Dempsey (1982) notes that collocation alone does not necessarily lead to cross-program staff communication, more appropriate referrals, or any other benefits beyond basic physical convenience. Finally, Austin (1982) notes that the simple collocation of services with diverse clienteles and programmatic intents may actually heighten interprogram conflict; disagreements over facility and maintenance costs may reinforce program fragmentation. The amalgam of these caveats indicates that although a potential facilitator of program coordination, collocation can realize its purported benefits only when accompanied by careful administrative planning and program linkages that go beyond physical location.

Information Systems

By establishing a centralized network for gathering, processing, and sharing data on clients, programs, and management issues, information systems can contribute toward the service integration goals of improved program management and increased accessibility, accountability, and service capability. In general, information systems can be divided into the two categories of *client information* and *organizational information,* with the former providing information in support of the service delivery process (such as referring clients to services, client tracking), and the latter focusing on information related to the internal workings and management (budgeting, planning, evaluation) of the organization or effort (Bowers and Bowers 1977).

Concentrating on client information systems, Bowers and Bowers (1977) have identified four subcategories: (1) social service information systems, focusing on a specific service type (day care, foster care); (2) information and referral systems, linking clients to services of all types within a community; (3) multiservice information systems, similar to information and referral but developed specifically to serve a multi-service center; and (4) target group information systems, serving a specific population, such as the handicapped or aged. Within each subcategory, the authors further note the specific stages in the service delivery process at which each system type is applicable (outreach, intake, diagnosis, and so on). This conception of client information systems is especially valuable for its ability to identify and delimit the components and scope of what is often cited as a particularly unwieldy strategy to implement, and in its success in relating the various categories of systems to the core functions of the service delivery process.

Data collected by organizational information systems on personnel, expenditures, and service delivery can contribute to improved program management, more informed resource allocations, improved service quality and efficiency, and increased accountability (National Academy of Public Administration 1977). Unlike client information systems, the characteristics of organizational information systems are not unique to the human service field but may be found in almost any well-run organization (Bowers and Bowers 1977), thereby allowing for much wider cross-fertilization of knowledge and techniques across fields.

Culling findings from past information system efforts, the literature has identified some general guidelines for the creation of successful information systems. The involvement of a "key person," politically savvy and able to commandeer sustainable resources, has often made the difference between success and failure. Also important is the involvement of all potential users in designing the system and in determining its output. Such engagement ensures maximum usefulness of the information system's data and creates a shared sense of ownership and commitment (Bowers and Bowers 1977). Indeed, it seems that information systems "survive only if all participating agencies derive some benefit from them" (Dempsey 1982, p. 106). On the other hand, information systems should use caution by including only that information necessary for achieving the service integration effort's goals, rather than *all* data desired or requested by involved parties, to avoid burdensome data collection and to facilitate identification of critical information by users of the information system (U.S. Department of Health and Human Services 1983). Addressing issues of program fragmentation and shared terminologies and creating a clear and accepted policy on confidentiality foster both program integration in general and the successful functioning of the information system (Bowers and Bowers 1977; U.S. Department of Health and Human Services 1983). Finally, reasonable expectations regarding the rate at which integrated information systems can be developed is critical, for it has been found that consolidating scores of data sets and information systems into a single system can take a great deal of time and effort. An early estimate in Florida was five years (National Academy of Public Administration 1977), and Michigan took four years and millions of dollars to implement a limited demonstration (Dempsey 1982). Although advancements in computer technology have certainly speeded the development of information systems, it is clear from the experience of the integrated Department of Health and Rehabilitative Services in Florida that premature demands for an integrated and expanded data base by legislative committees, federal agencies, and headquarters staff can cripple implementation efforts while they are still in their infancy (National Academy of Public Administration 1977).

Integrated Staffing

In integrated staffing, programs join to make collective decisions on staff management issues, including the reassignment and sharing of staff across programs. Gans and Horton (1975) examined these linkages in their evaluation of 30 integration projects and were able to identify five categories of strategies: (1) consolidated personnel administration (including hiring, firing, promoting, and training), (2) joint use of staff (two or more agencies using the same staff to deliver services), (3) staff transfer (moving an employee from one agency to another), (4) staff collocation, and (5) staff outstationing (placing staff from one service provider in the facility of another). Such manipulation of staff can be extremely difficult unless the integrator holds authority over providers (as by control of funding) or can provide some incentive to provider participation. This is especially true in the case of staff transferral, which "strikes at the heart of agency authority" (Gans and Horton 1975, p. 106). It should be noted, however, that coercion is not the only route to integrated staffing; for example, the joint use of staff may arise from a heightened awareness of the functions of other agencies and a desire to reduce duplication.

In the Gans and Horton (1975) study, the use of outstationing and collocation of staff was found to increase accessibility and efficiency by moving a wider range of services closer to client groups. Efficiency was further increased by minimizing duplication, and the improved communication and understanding among providers generated by staffing linkages facilitated greater continuity in service delivery. No effects were discerned from the consolidation of staff hiring, firing, or promotion authority.

Joint Planning and Programming

Conducted by coordinating committees and other interprogram bodies, joint planning and programming enable the generation of (1) agreed-upon assessments of needs and priorities, (2) guidelines for the administration of the integrative effort, and (3) programmatic proposals to meet the effort's service objectives. Though the most frequently used integrative technique found in a study of 12 HEW-funded service integration projects (Sampson, 1971), joint planning and programming linkages require specific conditions concerning the authority of participating individuals and the inclusion of involved parties. For example, those taking part in such linkages must (1) have administrative authority in their home agencies in order to implement decisions, (2) represent clinical as well as administrative domains to enable the creation of appropriate and effective programmatic solutions, and (3) represent the full array of service providers involved in the effort. As is the case in collocation, this third prerequisite can draw out established animosities among providers (Gans and Horton 1975) but also may serve as a forum for the improvement of poor relations that would otherwise continue unaddressed.

Regarding its specific outcomes, joint planning and programming can improve the continuity of service delivery by identifying and closing gaps in service and by allowing providers to plan services in a complementary manner. The joint selection of central support staff can allow more legitimate, and thus more effective, interprovider liaisons. Finally, such linkages can reduce duplication of service and can achieve economies of scale through coordinated programming (Gans and Horton 1975).

Fiscal Linkages

The last type of program-centered integrative strategy is fiscal linkages, in which the coordinated use of funds can create and strengthen links among providers, develop and expand services, and lead to more comprehensive service delivery. Three of the more common linkages are (1) purchase of services, (2) joint budgeting, and (3) joint funding (including pooled funding).

Purchase of services. This strategy, in which the integrator organization uses its project funds to purchase services from providers who can render a needed service most efficiently, can—if funds are sufficient—place the integrator in a strong bargaining position. In exchange for the increase in business, provider participation in other integrating activities can be required. In addition to furnishing additional services for clients, providers may be bound to alter the content of service, develop new services, participate in joint programming with other providers, or share confidential information in support of an integrated information system (Gans and Horton 1975). The effectiveness of this strategy increases when the integrator is the source of substantial or pooled funds (see below). On the other hand, as noted in the discussion of barriers in chapter 8, the political viability and effectiveness of this strategy may be curtailed if the integrator is itself a direct provider of services.

Purchase of services may have an additional impact at the client-centered level of service integration. If purchasing and case management are housed within the same entity (the integrator), some amount of client voice in the provision of services may be established. By collectively expressing clients' satisfaction with particular services, case managers' reports can influence the distribution of integrator funds among providers, thus creating a client-oriented locus of accountability for services (Community Life Association 1974).

Joint budgeting. Although pledging to contour resource allocation to the greatest needs (ideally, as prioritized through joint planning), joint budgeting can be undermined by providers' reluctance to relinquish their rights to budget determination. The promise of additional dollars for participants can help overcome this reluctance. But when the promise falls through, as was the case at the HUB Service Center in Cincinnati, interest in joint budgeting quickly falls away (Gans and Horton 1975).

Joint funding. In joint funding, at its most basic, two or more providers contribute funds to support a service. Eliciting this activity is often attractive to integration projects because it serves as an in-kind fulfillment of the local share often required by federal funding. If pursued further, however, joint funding can also serve to reform, rather than simply augment, the delivery of services. For example, joint funding may be used to provide a comprehensive, cross-program outreach service, thereby increasing client accessibility to a wider range of services (Gans and Horton 1975).

Pooled funding, in which the integrator collects dollars from providers and then redistributes them on a greatest-need basis, is another example. Such funds may be collected from local matches of public funds, such as Title IV-A (Gans and Horton 1975), or, as was the case in the Hartford (Conn.) SITO demonstration, from direct contributions from public, nonprofit, and foundation sources (Community Life Association 1974).

The potential benefits of pooled funding are many, especially when the pool represents the bulk of service funds. In such an arrangement, the integrator is better able to respond quickly to sudden needs for services with specifically targeted funds. Information on each service unit in a client's service plan can be tracked easily, facilitating determination of the cost-benefits of a given plan. Discretion in the distribution of funds facilitates joint planning and management activities by the involved parties. And in relation to the policy-centered level of integration, the benefits realized by pooled funding can attract dollars that would ordinarily be targeted to specific programs (Community Life Association 1974).

Despite its promise, however, pooled funding faces considerable attitudinal and systemic barriers. Issues of turf and self-preservation may cause program administrators to view any alteration in their financing system with trepidation. Further, without policy-level reform, freedom in the use of pooled funds remains restricted by narrow eligibility criteria and other regulations that accompany many funding streams.

Policy-Centered Integration

As program-centered strategies foster a more holistic perspective of service provision, so policy-centered strategies work to create a comprehensive, problem-oriented philosophy of policy creation that transcends the categorical perspectives of current policy-making. Strategies at this level (1) tend to involve intergovernmental groups, which operate above the categorical boundaries that divide human services and are responsible, through the membership of elected officials, directly to the public interest, and (2) support the creation of integrative human service policy to effect reform at the program and client levels.

Intergovernmental Organizations

Often called interdepartmental boards, policy advisory councils, human service cabinets and commissions, or interagency task forces, intergovernmental organizations provide a broadly representative forum for the heads of agencies, elected officials, and (often) nonprofit service providers and foundations to identify the needs of a given community and prescribe integrative policy solutions. Created at the local level and the state level (where it is often lodged in the governor's office), these units vary greatly in their authority and tasks, ranging from advising governors on the shortcomings of the fragmented service system, to collating information on all legislation (and their regulations) affecting human services, to developing comprehensive state human service budgets to identify service gaps and set policy priorities (Dempsey 1982; Division of State Planning and Community Affairs 1974; Mudd 1982). Because of their position above categorical divisions and the membership in them of elected officials, they may serve as a central locus of accountability, answerable to the citizenry for the delivery of human services and the improvement of clients' lives. Especially when equipped with financial support, some authority over agencies, and program oversight (Bruner 1989a), they can also improve human services by conducting needs assessments, setting policy priorities, and monitoring and evaluating programs and services (National League of Cities/U.S. Conference of Mayors 1974). Further, they need not take on the full brunt of the reform effort in order to be supportive; in some cases, the best action may be simply to assume a clearly defined, "arm's length" policy role (Hawkins 1977; cited in Agranoff and Pattakos 1979).

Though intergovernmental groups afford a locus for centralized accountability, a noncategorical perspective, and the capacity for policy reform, their involvement in the creation of integrative policy exposes the initiative to temporary commitments occasioned by the uncertain tenure of elected officials. These officials may view service coordination as an additional layer of government and an increased tax burden (Research Group 1973), and thus as not politically worthy of a long-term commitment.

Funding Strategies

With the potential for considerable influence over legislation, state and local budgets, and existing regulations, policy-centered service integration provides powerful strategic mechanisms for accessing funding across service areas. Such funding strategies include appropriating dollars to support an infrastructure for coordinating services and accessing additional resources, taking fuller advantage of available federal resources via refinancing, and decategorizing current funding streams for social services.

Supporting a service integration infrastructure. Funding to establish a core infrastructure for service integration efforts—thus providing the staff and capacity to integrate services and coordinate additional resources—may be difficult to achieve because it is often viewed as a precursor to requests for additional service and integration-support dollars (see chapter 8). Such targeted funding, however, has been cited as an important element in facilitating service integration (Farrow and Joe 1992; Yessian 1991) and is used to establish and/or provide additional support to family resource centers, school-based service centers, and other organizations or individuals charged with coordinating services for clients. Dollar amounts for this purpose need not be large. In the case of Kentucky's Education Reform Act of 1989, the state legislature called for the establishment of Family Resource and Youth Service Centers in schools serving lower-income populations and provided the centers with deliberately small funds ($10,000 to $90,000 per site) with the intent of spurring more creative and aggressive coordination of existing resources (Farrow and Joe 1992). Thus, though it might represent only limited financial commitments, targeted support for an integration infrastructure can lead to greater leverage of existing resources and improved service integration.

Refinancing. Given the current tangle of federal funding streams and regulations, using such sources to their maximum advantage requires creativity and invention. One particularly promising method of accessing greater federal support is by refinancing, in whole or in part, the share of services currently paid for by state and local dollars (such as health care, education, and child welfare) with federal resources, thereby freeing state and local funds for use in service integration. One example of this strategy is the refinancing of some special education services, including physical, speech, and occupational therapies, with Medicaid dollars; a variety of school health services may also be at least partially reimbursable by Medicaid. But Medicaid refinancing should not be considered a cash cow: it is often subject to strict regulations concerning funded services—running contrary to service integration goals—as well as a reluctance among state Medicaid offices and federal officials to support extensive Medicaid expansion (Farrow and Joe 1992).

Decategorization. Allowing greater discretion in the use of funds at both the policy and program/provider levels, the decategorization of human service funding is an ambitious strategy with a profound impact on service system reform. Categorical funding systems often prejudge the needs of clients by prescribing both the amount of money and the way in which a provider may use it. Clients with special needs are then forced to navigate the maze of categorical regulations to access services—a task that has been compared to "trying to fit a square peg into a round hole" (Kusserow 1991, p. A-13). Decategorization breaks down these restrictive barriers among funding sources, allowing the flexibility to program service plans around the specific needs of individuals. Furthermore, decategorization can also foster a willingness among providers to view client service as a shared task (Kusserow 1991). An instructive example of this strategy: in 1988 Iowa instituted a decategorized Child Welfare Fund in two counties, eliminating eligibility and other categorical restrictions in 32 separate child welfare funding sources. This effort has facilitated a focus on preventive services to avoid more expensive long-term care (Bruner 1989a) and has allowed local child welfare committees greater discretion in the types of services they provided.

Organizationally Centered Integration

Organizationally centered strategies involve the reorganization of governmental structures to facilitate the execution of strategies in the other three domains (Agranoff and Pattakos 1979). Often referred to as umbrella agencies or departments of human resources or human services, the products of these activities involve the restructuring of the human service system to incorporate formerly independent agencies (such as welfare, health, mental health, and corrections) under a single new organizational entity. This restructuring then provides the foundation for, but no guarantee of, further integration efforts at the program and policy levels. Indeed, when not backed up by reform in other domains, such reorganization may simply be a front for agency expansion or, alternately, a placebo for change to assuage reform advocates.

Reorganization and the Creation of Umbrella Agencies

More than half the states have organizations that combine a variety of public assistance and social services. Each of these organizations includes at least three of the following: public health, mental health, mental retardation, adult corrections, youth institutions, vocational rehabilitation, and employment services (Chi 1987). Similar departments exist at the local level as well, with half the counties with populations over 50,000 and one fourth of all cities having departments combining two or more domains (Agranoff and Pattakos 1989; Agranoff 1988).

Despite their popularity, no two umbrella agencies are alike. Although diagrams of their internal organization may be similar, their structures provide only a framework for idiosyncratic conglomerations of integrative activities in the policy and program (including administration) domains, as well as unique balances of centralized authority and programmatic autonomy, and variation in the formality of linkages (Agranoff and Pattakos 1979).

The concept that reorganization of the human service system is a foundation for additional, or rather more direct, integrative efforts is cited repeatedly in the literature (Agranoff and Pattakos 1979; Dempsey 1982; Levinson and Hutchinson 1973; Sampson 1971). Dempsey notes that reorganization "does not automatically lead to improved coordination of service delivery, but it does, in part, remove a major barrier thereto, namely turf" (1982, pp. 102–103). Agranoff and Pattakos suggest that "structural change is designed to create new *opportunities for change*" (1979, p. 130, emphasis added).

Support for this assertion comes from a National Academy of Public Administration report on Florida's Department of Health and Rehabilitative Services, perhaps the most studied example of an umbrella agency, which states that "the reorganization laid a sound organizational basis for services integration" (1977, p. 1). In its description of the effort's highlights and low points, the study looks beyond the reorganization process and describes specific strategies that—from our four-domain perspective of integrative strategies—fall under the program and policy domains: the success of collocation, deficiencies in information systems, the need for stricter hiring standards, and so forth. These were the elements that shaped the department's experience.

This is not to belittle the task of creating an umbrella agency, which can be a difficult, prolonged, and politicized process (Briar 1982), nor to ignore the existence of a variety of organizational structures that can be applied to a reorganization effort, with consequent influence on the experience of the reform effort. For example, the Council on State Governments has classified three categories of reorganized human service agencies (defined in chapter 7): coordinated, consolidated, and integrated (Council of State Governments 1974). In addition, matrix models of human service system reorganization have been promoted as improved organizationally centered integration strategies (see chap. 6, above; also Curtis 1976; Reagan 1987, cited in Agranoff 1991).

Rather, the distinction between reorganization and program- and policy-centered strategies in umbrella agencies serves to clarify the scope and capacity of each type of integrative strategy in the process. Because the creation of umbrella agencies is a high-profile and easily politicized activity (usually falling under the authority of elected executives) and thus subject to widespread scrutiny, its failure to measure up to the expectations of the public or of various constituencies may lead to placing full blame for any shortcomings of the integration effort on the act of reorganization itself. Writing off reorganization as merely shuffling boxes, however, may in some cases reflect unfamiliarity with the various levels of activity that are required in service integration and indicate that certain expectations have been placed on the wrong integrative strategy (Agranoff and Pattakos 1979). In the other cases, however, in which integration efforts are focused exclusively on reorganization strategies without regard for reform in the other domains, such criticism may well be justified.

Reorganization at the Local and County Level

Although the bulk of attention has been focused on state-level efforts, statistics cited above indicate that organizational reform has been a popular strategy in cities and counties as well. Local reorganizational initiatives in the 1970s have resulted in such entities as the Dade County (Fla.) Department of Human Resources and the Dallas Office of Human Development, as well as organizations coordinated from the chief executive's office, such as those in Dayton and New Orleans. The scope of these efforts has ranged from community action to the inclusion of public health and welfare functions (Agranoff and Pattakos 1979). Incorporating not only program areas but the services themselves, the Kalamazoo County (Mich.) Human Service Department initiated a process that includes the creation of a program umbrella, the consolidation of support services, and the development of a new program structure in which all services are grouped under the four categories of prevention, treatment, human development, and health protection (Vander Schie, Wagenfeld, and Worgess 1987, cited in Agranoff 1991).

The division of service integration strategies into the four categories of client-centered, program-centered, policy-centered, and organizationally centered integration contributes a more refined conceptual perspective of service integration than the more common and less specific service/system or service delivery/program administration dichotomies. Using it as the framework for this discussion of service integration strategies suggests that these four domains also have practical utility. They enable planners to define more specifically the goals of service integration efforts and suggest specific strategies more closely matched to achieving the prescribed outcomes.

Part IV
Putting the Past to Work for the Future

10

Implications: Understanding the Past

Service integration is neither a new construct nor one that has yielded the kinds of outcomes that had been anticipated. Commonly, such lack of success is attributed primarily to the barriers discussed in chapter 8. While recognizing their import, this analysis suggests that it is not these barriers alone that have impeded implementation. Rather, fundamental assumptions that have historically undergirded our thinking about, and our approaches to, service integration have unwittingly contributed to the limited pace of successful implementation. These assumptions, discussed below, represent an almost silent evolution of ideas that were tacitly and sometimes unknowingly passed on by those concerned with service enhancement. They were not embraced consciously or universally, but they form the historic undercurrent on which service integration efforts rode—and which predicted their course.

Assumption I: What's Good for the Agency Is Good for the Client

This assumption suggests that most service integration efforts confounded both in theory and in practice the impact of the initiative on the client and on the agency. Inherent in this assumption are two parallel themes, one ideological and one practical. Ideologically, it was felt that the implementation of service integration would serve a common good, that what was good for one was good for all. Service integration would in all cases be benign at worst. Its negative consequences were rarely considered. Service integration—though discussed in the literature—was not so clearly delineated in practice. Client ends became confounded with agency ends. Goals were confused, and means and ends were mixed up. The few practical frameworks that had been developed to differentiate among goals, and between methods and outcomes, gathered dust on bookshelves, isolated from the action of service integration.

The Common Good

Men come easily to believe that arrangements agreeable to themselves are beneficial to others.

A fool can put on his own clothes better than a wise man can do it for him.
(Olshansky 1973, p. 203)

Though the word *empowerment* rang through the community action efforts of the 1960s, fertile work in service integration of the 1970s and 1980s tended to minimize such a client-empowerment orientation. The client's voice, though acknowledged, was not predominant. Services were being integrated to meet client need, but the planning and strategies used clearly favored the expertise and engagement of service practitioners and professionals working within the system. Clients, if

From Past to Future

involved, were there to reinforce the momentum of change rather than to redirect it.

Olshansky (1973), writing about vocational education and rehabilitation, noted the overwhelming power of extant systems to socialize workers and clients. "Anyone working within a system becomes more or less blinded by it. That the blinding process does not always become apparent to many of its victims does suggest how effective the process can be" (p. 203). Although the central goal of service integration may have been to alter relationships and perhaps tilt the balance of power between agencies and service providers, little attention was paid to power realignment among clients and providers. The assumption was that by inserting new practices, mechanisms, and outreach strategies, reform at the client level would ensue and outcomes improve. Neither was much attention given in these early efforts to altering human relations. The wielders of power were seduced into believing that a focus on strategic change as opposed to a change in relations would alter outcomes.

Efforts to realign power to the client were considered subordinate to—or at most equated with—bettering the system. Himmelman (1991) provides the clearest enunciation of the differences between betterment (of the system) and empowerment (of the individual). Betterment models—which characterize many past service integration efforts—are initiated by large and influential institutions in control of their governance and administration. Staff members are responsible to the institution, and though they seek advice from target communities or clients, they are not accountable to these groups. In contrast, the empowerment approach is initiated in a community setting and is assisted by community organization. Community and client priorities are reflected at the outset through a process of mutual goal setting, where substantial emphasis is placed on balancing the needs of clients and the system. Power is shared among those involved.

When one maps the reality of service integration initiatives against these contrasting approaches, it is apparent that although profoundly concerned with positively affecting client outcomes, early service integration efforts rarely focused on empowering client voice or on realigning power relationships among clients and providers. In contrast, efforts focused, for example, on developing common definitions, using standardized forms, and altering patterns of service provision. However well intentioned, they failed to acknowledge that what was good for the system—what promoted efficiency—could unwittingly exploit clients. The assumption of a common good obliterated the reality that systemic hegemony can deny client power and can obstruct client growth—that it can defeat the very purpose that justifies its existence.

Confusing Ends and Means

In part, then, insufficient success of historic approaches to service integration can be attributed to insufficient delineation of goals, manifest in the sometimes erroneous equation that what is good for the agency is good for the client.

But the dilemma does not end there. Although elegant taxonomies exist in the literature, they have not been translated into reality. By replacing the common conception of service integration as a singular, global entity with subdivided, domain-based models (e.g., Agranoff and Pattakos 1979), frameworks can facilitate the delineation of clear and circumscribed goals, the distinction between goal and process, and the selection of appropriate and specific strategies to meet desired ends. These same frameworks, however, have failed to be put into practice, leaving service integrators without the conceptual precision to make the integration fully realizable. As a result, short-term strategies, insufficient to address the complex problems to which service integration should be directed, are the norm. In the case of the Allied Services Act, for example, opponents of the act, some of whom in fact supported service integration, deplored the proposals for their limited focus on administrative integration (Redburn 1977). Without the guidance of clear frameworks, therefore, practitioners are forced to reinvent the wheel, often globalizing their intents and thereby rendering them of limited utility.

Indeed, the globalization of service integration efforts is increasingly being rejected in favor of crisper efforts that delineate means and specify clear ends. Agranoff and Pattakos (1979) conclude their definitive analysis of service integration with one admonition: "*At the risk of sounding overly simplistic, it is extremely crucial that services integration strategists closely ponder what and why they are integrating. Indeed, careful consideration of such questions from the very beginning of integration efforts may prove to be the single most important factor behind success*" (pp. 160–161; emphasis in original). Yessian (1991), in his twenty-year review of service integration, recommends that service integration strategies focus on well-defined target groups and pursue reform within tightly specified domains. It is argued that such a strategy facilitates greater precision in setting priorities and in assessing performance. All that we have learned demands clear goals that disentangle what is good for the client, what is good for the agency, and what is good for the system.

Assumption II: Service Integration Is Everybody's and Nobody's Responsibility

The history of service integration is characterized by a revolving-door approach to leadership. Early on, responsibility for comprehensive planning for service coordination was lodged in the private sector, with much of the work taking place at the local level. As government engagement in the human services and categorical programs expanded, the federal government became increasingly engaged in comprehensive planning. Various approaches to federalism coincided with the evolution of service integration, with Nixon's New Federalism having the most profound effect on the field. With New Federalism's stated focus on general purpose governments and its commitment to the devolution of authority to the states, the prevailing sentiment—that which framed and initiated many of the service integration efforts of the 1970s— seemed to accord increasing responsibility to the states. Localities were to be engaged as well, though roles were not clearly delineated.

Implications

With little federal initiative on service integration in the 1980s, despite an increasing need for it, local initiatives, often undertaken with private or foundation support, began to flourish. In some communities, such efforts were lodged under the aegis of a private-sector agency; in other communities and states, mayoral or gubernatorial leadership provided for such initiatives within the executive branch.

Such episodic and wavering commitment to service integration has caused it to be everybody's and nobody's responsibility simultaneously. It has been suggested, for example, that during the 1970s the federal government, while advocating a strengthened role for the states, actually took the lead in shaping service integration strategies to meet its needs for efficiency and accountability. Despite some devolution of planning to the states, leadership for service integration was lodged at the federal level, making the 1970s an era of federal leadership on the issue. Yet, lacking similar leadership in the 1980s, service integration, to the degree that it was on the agenda, clearly became the purview of the states and localities.

Whether or not one accepts these delineations, service integration has been the theoretical hot potato, tossed among agencies and levels of government with alarming frequency. Indeed, the only certainty associated with service integration may be the uncertainty of its auspices and the brief duration of its ability to command public support. Agranoff (1986) notes that such inconsistency has led to the development of a set of activities created de novo in each locale with little strategic or policy support. Not only is there little sharing or cross-fertilization of strategy, but the lack of consistent policy support implies that such efforts are not worthy of sustenance. In this scenario, it appears that service integration is nobody's primary responsibility.

By contrast, and perhaps because it remains unassigned, service integration becomes everybody's added-on responsibility. Reforms arise from different systems, are anchored in different disciplines, and emanate from increasingly fragmented congressional jurisdictions, thus increasing the complexity of service integration. Taking the example of case management, Kahn and Kamerman (1992) write that agencies and organizations are often willing to cooperate with the service integration of others, but are reluctant to abandon any case management system previously established to address their own problems. At the client level, the result is that the family has multiple case managers; at the policy level, each program or service may be separately mandated to manage cases, prohibiting the elimination of case management from the agency's own repertoire of services; at the systems level, service replication— precisely what we have sought to avoid—is being perpetuated in the name of service integration.

To ameliorate this situation, systems reform is necessary across the spectrum of services, with clear delineation of roles and sufficient regulatory flexibility. Efforts of this sort are being undertaken—in Iowa, for example—and appear to be promising. It is evident, then, that without some overarching structure responsible for the oversight of service integration, categorical integration efforts will remain sporadic, isolated, and of limited effectiveness.

Deciding where and with whom to lodge leadership responsibility for service integration is problematic for several reasons. First, service integration as an operational construct remains an overlay on top of the existing categorical system. As such, it is a subject of interest to conflicting constituencies. Congress would be hard pressed to choose among categoricals because of the constituent support that each one enjoys. By contrast, service integration does not have strong, comprehensive constituent support to render guidance or to be offered as a replacement for the support categoricals enjoy.

Second, the current function and federalist structure of the U.S. governmental system gives us little clue as to where service integration should be lodged and what form it should take. Historically, as we have seen, our government vacillates on what its roles in service delivery should be at the federal, state, and local levels. Edelman and Radin (1991b) note that we have not resolved the "make it or buy it" question: whether government—state or local—should deliver services through their own providers (make it) or issue grants to accomplish its purposes (buy it). How this question is answered clearly influences the focus and locus of service integration efforts. Yet ambiguity prevails.

With little clarity concerning who is responsible for service integration, it is not surprising that its history seesaws between top-down and bottom-up strategies. Working exclusively at the operational level has resulted in inadequate support to sustain service integration efforts. Bottom-up strategies that have bypassed local bureaucracies (as in the Community Action Agency era) have been short-lived in terms of their contributions to service integration. Altman (1991), in an incisive critique, expresses concern "about community-based strategies as a main weapon in the fight against poverty in the decade ahead" (p. 79). Community intervention, which is so dependent on leadership and context, may not be viable in the very communities that need it most. At best, such strategies "bubbling up community by community" (Altman 1991) will be highly variable and difficult to maintain. Conversely, strategies that have focused solely on the state or national level have tended to remain distant from the realities of service integration. They have been labeled "subordinative," "mechanical," and "shallow" (Agranoff 1986). Indeed, a review of the history suggests that neither exclusively top-down nor bottom-up strategies have been effective service integration elixirs.

To resolve the top-down/bottom-up controversy, scholars and practitioners are making recommendations for an integration of approaches (Edelman and Radin 1991b). Emanating from many sectors, this two-tiered strategy has many names and theoretical justifications. Agranoff (1986) calls for a form of transorganizational management that emphasizes systems theory. He suggests invoking a "new paradigm . . . where the managerial task bridges the traditional structural components of a single organization authority structure" (p. 540). Although the precise practical elements of such a transorganizational structure are not yet clear, they transcend conventional hierarchical ordering and recognize the need for intermediate structures.

Alternatively, Bruner (1989b) suggests a concrete strategy that links "state" and "street" efforts. When states receive or appropriate dollars for service integration, they are able to direct the flow of activity and provide an incentive for action. Bruner suggests that this is a proper role for the state, with the caution that such incentives not be restricted by too stringent a prescription or regulatory constraints. Such incentives, he asserts, should be accompanied by supports for professional development and a call for clear client-centered objectives. He urges us to consider how state financing can be used to "replicate the unique; to institutionalize the noninstitutional; to mass produce human, one-to-one interactions" (Bruner 1989b, p. 5).

Advocating combined top-down/bottom-up strategies may seem as vague a position as the assumption that service integration is everybody's and nobody's business. In the sense that it dislodges sole responsibility from any one level of government, that is correct. Yet current work represents an advancement in that it is attempting to ferret out who is responsible for what; it does not beg the question of allocating responsibility. It suggests that for service integration to take hold with greater permanency and efficacy than we have seen, bottom-up and top-down strategies must be employed synergistically. One is not a replacement for the other. Indeed, conceiving community, state, and national strategies separately perpetuates the very dichotomies that service integration is working to alleviate.

Assumption III: The Impact of Service Integration Is Knowable and Measurable

Even the most cursory review of the service integration literature reveals that considerable attention has been paid to evaluating these disparate enterprises. Whether emanating from multidisciplinary strands of the 1970s or from the categorical efforts that followed, provisions for evaluation have existed. Indeed, this is one of the distinctive features of the service integration movement.

Spurred on by the legitimate need to inform practice, generate objective knowledge, and target federal expenditures to efforts that "work," formal evaluations were undertaken in the 1960s, though Lindblom and Cohen (1979) date the beginning of professional social inquiry to the early years of the century. Whatever the starting date, there is little question that additional funds for evaluation have been written into program authorizations since the 1960s. Moreover, an evaluation industry has mushroomed, with efforts centered in government, universities, and contract firms. Courses in evaluation are now taught, and constituencies for evaluation have evolved. The science of speaking "truth to power" has arisen.

But despite the growth of the evaluation industry, arguments over the value of such an enterprise abound. Kimmel (1981) cites countless analyses wherein the conclusions about formal evaluations are gloomy and disappointing. Schmidt, Scanlon, and Bell (1979) note that program evaluation has not led to successful policies and programs; on the contrary, it has been isolated from federal decision making and has produced little information of interest and utility to policymakers. Pincus (1980) suggests that evaluation efforts have been exercises in miscommunication, in which neither party understands the premises of the other. Writing more recently, Schorr (1989) and Crowson and Boyd (1992) affirm the lack of hard evaluation evidence. There is little doubt that an empirical void exists, and that efforts to use data to guide policy have met with only limited success.

In part, the lack of success is attributed to inherent values and expectations that color all evaluation efforts and limit their objectivity. Values are expressed in the selection of programs to be evaluated, the choice of evaluators, the conduct of the evaluation, the analysis of results, and the inferences made in policy recommendations. Expectations come from the desire to separate the wheat from the chaff and to replicate the best efforts. Not limited to service integration, such expectations assume the generalizability of inputs and outputs, downplaying the importance of contextual and temporal variables, baseline capacity and expertise, and institutional support and political receptivity for the effort.

A particular challenge for service integration, generalizing from one locale to another or one level of government to another, has special heuristic appeal. Kimmel (1981) points out that our system of federalism invites little more than a trial-and-error approach to accumulating experience. With 50 states, hundreds of municipalities, and the federal government, we have many idiosyncratic laboratories for service integration. Such concerns are echoed in a study that compared integrated and categorical social services in Pennsylvania (American Public Welfare Association 1976). Beyond problems associated with geographic or contextual generalizability, Kimmel (1981) warns that more often than not, cumulative learning is the ideal; the reality is that policymakers at one level copy or mimic programs from another on the basis of hearsay, for political advantage. Claims for certain approaches run well ahead of their demonstrated efficacy, a caveat that applies to many a model or demonstration that designers hope will be replicated.

Even beyond these values and expectations, methodological issues also cloud service integration evaluation. Traditionally, formal evaluations require hypotheses, independent and dependent variables, and measures to test such hypotheses. At each turn, service integration presents a challenge to this process. To begin with, the sheer numbers and interactions of variables create an evaluation nightmare, especially in the light of the comparatively limited number of programs being examined. Solarz (1973), in setting forth a research paradigm on service integration, elaborates 23 independent variables, ranging from the integration of physical facilities and technical assistance to the commingling of categorical budgets. The very range of variables indicates the difficulties, as does the potential number of dependent variables, including performance levels of all personnel, performance behavior of clients, spouses, and children, organizational attitudes toward service integration, deinstitutionalization of clients, reduction in service delivery duplication, and client outcomes (decreased feelings of powerlessness and inadequacy, perception of access to services). The evaluation process can founder in a cacophony of mixed variables and limited adequate measures.

Further, even if the variables were more limited and the measures adequate, we would still be faced with the problem of attribution: to what specific intervention, or to which partner in the initiative, are specific outcomes attributable? (If the collaboration is truly a shared enterprise, it may well be impossible to settle attribution issues conclusively.) In sum, solid empirical frameworks to guide inquiry have been sparse, indeed.

With few definitive results emanating from the early work, analyses tried to become more descriptive and explanatory and to delineate practical barriers and change mechanisms. Over time, they also strove for greater sensitivity to the role of context, particularly political context. Many, rather than trying to provide an explanation of the entire array of service integration strategies, focused on one or two (such as information systems and case management). But though the type, form, and content of the evaluations changed over time, the spirit that motivated them remained constant—that the impact of service integration was knowable and measurable.

This assumption persisted despite the formidable complexities of interventions and despite the reality that knowledge of the problems service integration tried to ameliorate remained imprecise. Feild, D'Amico, and Benton (1978), in an evaluation of a unification project in Utah, wrote:

> The concept of service integration has long been regarded as the means by which to address some of the problems expressed by respondents in Utah. In theory, the proposed solutions sound reasonable. But it is impossible to measure the impact of a given intervention strategy without a clear understanding of the magnitude of the problems the strategy is intended to address. This has been the major limitation to most service integration projects: *we are unable to measure change because we haven't measured the problem.* (p. 22; emphasis added)

Indeed, it may not only be the case that we have not measured the problem; it may also be that we have not defined the intervention precisely enough to measure it. Kahn and Kamerman (1992) note that in the 1970s much of the service integration work focused on central-level or administrative-level consolidation or coordination, whereas more recent efforts seem to be regrouping around case-oriented integration of service delivery. In pointing out these differences, they acknowledge not only a changing orientation but also the need to circumscribe the focus of service integration into more manageable units. Their work suggests a cluster or partialization strategy that separates units by category (for instance, means-tested programs that offer money and resources, services for adolescents, or services for families with children under age 12). Whether these are the appropriate clusters warrants investigation; it is clear, however, that crisper units of analysis, clearer statements of the problem, and far clearer specification of outcomes are needed if we are going to realize the assumption that the impact of service integration is knowable and measurable.

Similarly, Morrill (1991a)—and earlier McLaughlin (1980), who criticized the logic of our inquiry (our preoccupation with scientism) and called for new and valid ways of knowing—reminds us that we need to make decisions regarding the means versus the ends of service integration. Kahn and Kamerman (1992) call for discerning processes related to service integration—organizational, interorganizational, and political issues, costs, and benefits—from the impacts of service integration—the actual outcomes for children and families. Similarly, Kagan, Rivera, Brigham, and Rosenblum (1992) call for distinguishing among different types of results: (1) *accomplishments,* which represent the fruition of process intentions, and (2) *outcomes,* which represent the quantifiable changes in the behavior, performance, or life conditions of those involved in service integration.

Though helpful, this two-tiered strategy remains insufficiently precise. It needs to be wedded to Agranoff and Pattakos's (1979) definitional hierarchy, giving clear voice to differentiating the intents of service integration: client-centered integration, program-centered integration, policy-centered integration, and organizationally centered integration. Within each domain, accomplishments and outcomes (processes and impacts) need to be discerned.

Further, such analyses must be linked directly to expenditures, yet this is difficult. Skeptics charge that service integration efforts deflect dollars from direct services themselves. Evaluation and cost-benefit evaluation is just one more step removed from direct service delivery. In general, however, service integration dollars tend to be very small in comparison to the investments already being made in our service delivery system for young children and families. Moreover, while we have spent decades trying to assess the cost-benefit ratios of various separate interventions, we have not been willing to put service integration efforts to similar tests that evaluate benefits over time or that take preventive savings into account. As Morrill has noted (1991b), "to the extent that collaborations are effective in cutting down long-term dependencies and performance shortfalls, the cost benefits could well justify additional expenditures. It would seem well worth exploring the potential" (p. 13).

Finally, the refined evaluation paradigm called for by McLaughlin (1980) needs development. Those concerned about turning the assumptions of measurability into the reality of measurability will have to grapple with definitional issues, measurement strategies, and assigning accountability to the collective implementors of service integration. Agranoff (1986) sums it up well, suggesting that the creative structures that are being established to implement service integration—collaborations, work teams, "ad-hocracies"—need to be matched by the same creativity and freshness of evaluation perspectives. He suggests that any effort to understand intergovernmental activity should be couched in understandings of legal and jurisdictional accommodations, and that intergovernmental research can and should shed light on interorganizational structures. In short, Agranoff may be suggesting that the field of service integration, rather than setting off on its own course of evaluation, link up with disciplines concerned with related issues.

Whatever the strategy employed, it is clear that past evaluation strategies need significant retooling. The assumption that the impact of service integration is knowable and measurable is not wrong; it is simply naively optimistic, given the current state of empirical strategies.

Assumption IV: Service Integration Is an Operationally Conservative, Strategically Benign Intervention That Can Reform Service Delivery and System Efficiency

A review of the literature on service integration reveals a mismatch of intent and strategy. The intent of service integration was framed by the idealism and hope of the 1960s, the bald expectation that America could and should do better by its young children and families, particularly if they were poor and burdened with multiple problems. Inside the frame, the silent reality underlying service integration in the 1960s and 1970s was that the system was out of control and, by the 1980s, that social problems were as well.

Edelman and Radin (1991a) view the dilemma through a temporal lens, suggesting that in the 1960s people believed there was a silver bullet, a magical solution to all ills, if only they could find it. Jumping from one solution to the next, never lighting long enough to put any strategy to the test, the 1960s perceptions lingered into the 1970s before giving way to those of the 1980s, which were sadly characterized by disillusionment—the belief that nothing works. Though Edelman and Radin do not use the term, they seem to suggest that the 1990s is the age of realism, that the myth of the silver bullet has been put to rest but hope tempered by humility persists. Put the lessons to use, we are told: this is the era of action.

As a consequence, advice on successful strategies abounds: avoid single model programs, secure durable funding, create shared leadership, formulate clear goals, create mini-city halls, follow top-down/ bottom-up strategies. Fine compilations of knowledge from practice and research are appearing (Mattessich and Monsey 1992; Melaville and Blank 1991). Conferences are being held (Blank and Lombardi 1992), and federal institutes are being developed.

The United States is experiencing a resurgence of the optimism that characterized the 1960s but is adding well-honed strategies to the brew. The question to be considered is whether such a strategy-driven approach is sufficient to the four domains of service integration identified by Agranoff and Pattakos (1979). By adopting a strategy-based agenda, are we (1) directing our efforts to all domains with equal likelihood of success, (2) delimiting or enhancing the chances for success, (3) being sufficiently inventive in our approaches to the challenge of integrating services, and (4) acknowledging the liabilities as well as the potentialities of service integration?

To date, with few exceptions, syntheses of the past literature have extracted the practical how-to's. Although these are helpful codifications and are particularly useful to the field, even if followed to the letter they remain conservative strategies: necessary, but insufficient to meet the task at hand. If we have learned anything from the past, it is the enormity of the service integration challenge and the need for radical and integrated reform to make this construct take root. Indeed, perhaps the appropriate question is, Is it reasonable to pursue a strategic agenda that does not encompass a philosophically rooted approach to service integration?

In examining service integration through the educational lens, Crowson and Boyd (1992) note that it is precisely the ingrained structures of schools—professional role interpretations, fundamental modes of operation—that have been largely unaffected by service integration efforts to date. They suggest that service integration must take bold steps; it must examine the possible "importance of changing governance structures in schools to better support services integration" (p. 35).

Echoing this sentiment, Gardner (1991a), an astute observer-participant of service integration over the decades, captures the magnitude of the challenge in discussing the funding of service integration: "Efforts to manipulate and massage a welter of funding streams into coherent delivery packages via partnerships or in multiservice centers are not enough. However successful individually, they simply cannot be ginned up to the scale necessary to make a dent in the numbers of children and families who need a better shot at success" (p. 16). Gardner, in rejecting a patchwork strategy, calls for nothing short of "radical reform in the design of funding streams" (p. 16), the specification of outcome accountability, and a revamped governance structure.

Beyond piecemeal, conservative reform, service integration needs to become more integrated, more coordinated and unitary. Reflecting this orientation, Edelman and Radin (1991a) suggest a "saturation strategy," where a single neighborhood of concentrated poverty would be engaged in planning and implementing a comprehensive strategy that would address housing, health care, mental health care, and family services. Such an approach would embrace the intention of service integration—namely, the full and comprehensive integration of services.

One example of this approach was the 21st Century Communities Initiative proposed by the Department of Health and Human Services, which was designed to improve services in 20 low-income communities through a comprehensive strategy of economic and social development efforts working together. In this plan, which was not implemented, government, the private sector, and local community organizations would have woven new initiatives in job creation, wage supplementation, job training, comprehensive school readiness efforts, and family and neighborhood support. Using a neighborhood-based family support structure, integrated approaches to planning, service delivery, and financing across funding streams were to be implemented (U.S. Department of Health and Human Services 1992).

Other comprehensive strategies have been suggested that embrace local, state, and federal initiatives, with some focused on planning, some on service delivery, and some on evaluation. Such efforts need to be comprehensively planned and broadly supported by the community and by professionals, a marriage that has eluded many past service integration efforts.

Finally, most research, theory building, and action assume that service integration will yield some positive results. Taking a systemic and more actively revolutionary approach to change demands that future work also examine the negative and nonneutral sequelae of

Implications   **177** service integration. Our preoccupation with potential merits must be balanced by an honest assessment of liabilities.

Such honest stock-taking, coupled with integrated reform, will not come easily or without supports. Many efforts are currently under way. In the next chapter, we turn to the future of service integration and examine what needs to be done to implement a renewed, robust service integration movement.

11

Recommendations: Looking to the Future

In the late 1980s and early 1990s, service integration has again risen to prominence. In this chapter we examine how recent efforts differ from and draw on past experiences, and we make recommendations regarding specific strategies that could help service integration become a more durable and effective construct.

The Present and the Past: Similarities and Differences

Because the history of service integration is long and rich, though marked by different strategic emphases, it has generated a distinctive culture. To be sure, like all cultures it has been modified by an accumulation of inputs along the way, including formidable contextual factors: vacillating federalisms, worsening social conditions of children and families, and an increasingly complex sociopolitical apparatus at the state and federal levels. Nonetheless, through the 1980s service integration followed a fairly predictable course. That was to change in the late 1980s and early 1990s. Though rooted in its historic culture, this latest version of service integration differs from past efforts in significant ways. Understanding *how* it differs is a prerequisite for understanding the recommendations that follow. Essentially, the movement is at a critical juncture, ready to go forward to more visionary and comprehensive thinking.

Changes in Attitudes

The first difference between past and current service integration efforts is manifest in a decreasing optimism regarding the viability of social reform. The service integration efforts of the 1970s were profoundly optimistic in their intent. Though rejecting the notion of community control, 1970s efforts did not give up in their pursuit of change. Maintaining their beliefs in the viability of government as a vehicle of social change, they sought other strategies to achieve comparable goals. Having seen Watts and Detroit burn, and having tasted the bitterness of social injustice, they wanted to redress social inequity and enhance governmental efficiency simultaneously. A sense that service integration involved strategic alteration, not fundamental reconceptualization, persisted through the years, framing a durable strategic and somewhat atheoretical approach to service integration.

Affirming the sense of diminished optimism and increased challenge that has emerged, Halpern (1991) suggests that "each wave of service reform in the United States has faced greater challenges than its predecessors" (p. 360). He notes that each successive iteration of reform has had to bear the burden of the "residue of half-developed or semiabandoned ideas" (p. 360). With theorists no longer bubbling with optimism, 1990s reform efforts have been born in the context of lost faith and discontent with the current social service structure.

Changes in Locus

A second major difference between service integration efforts of the 1970s and those of the present is that diminished optimism in general has been accompanied by diminished faith in the federal government as the sole catalyst for change. Aided initially by the ideology of the various federalisms and later by concerns over the ineffectiveness of the federal government, the locus of momentum for social change shifted from the federal to local and state levels. Heretofore, change, rather than being a grass-roots phenomenon, was the result of the establishment of higher standards at higher levels of government, including the Supreme Court and Congress (Capoccia 1973). With the advent of the proposals of the Allied Services Act and other legislation of the era, there was a shift to the states, at least on paper. But even then, it must be remembered, the designers of devolution strategies were federal bureaucrats. Though power was devolved for implementation purposes to the states, the federal government remained the service integration engineer. Service integration took on the veneer of local and state engagement because many of the efforts were instituted at those levels.

By contrast, recent efforts at service integration have far more of a local flavor, with impetus, planning, and support coming from states, municipalities, the private sector, and professional organizations. Communities throughout America have launched local and state collaborative efforts—more than 350 in the early childhood domain alone (Kagan, Rivera, and Lamb-Parker 1991). No longer the absent player, the private sector has (recalling early American history) become intimately involved in service integration efforts—sometimes as initiators and sometimes as funders. Moreover, increased private-sector involvement has been accompanied by federal expenditures on service integration. And new leadership in the White House, under President Clinton and Vice President Gore—leadership with a fervent desire to streamline government—may bode well for new service integration efforts.

The movement from the federal to the state and local level, and from public-sector to combined public/private-sector engagement,

however, is not without consequences. In an effort to propagate successful strategies, the replicated-model approach to practice and even to
policy, however criticized in theory, has been employed. Presently, federal legislation—and accompanying dollars—seems to be passed primarily when a model has been proven effective at the state level. But
such models, though working in one context, do not always transplant
well to other environments. Yet recognizing that this has become the
operative policy vehicle to replication and expanded reputation, program developers seek this route, each propagating unique (and sometimes contradictory) federal legislation. Not always negative, such a
strategy can work when developers recognize that strict fidelity to any
given model inhibits successful replication and when they build in flexibility and supports. The United Way's Success by Six effort is one such
example of a community-based approach to service integration and
systemic change that, while spawning a national strategy, encourages
local variation.

States and localities are taking the lead in this approach; mean-
while, the federal role, though diminished, is not nonexistent. As we
have noted earlier, categorical legislation has called for service integration strategies through the formation of state- and local-level councils. Moreover, the Department of Health and Human Services has
supported the National Center for Service Integration in establishing
a clearinghouse and providing technical and analytic support to the
emerging field. Support for the development of technical assistance
capacities has been accompanied by renewed federal emphasis on making waivers available so as not to quash state and local ingenuity. In
short, the momentum for 1990s service integration is—in contrast to
past eras—clearly lodged at the local and state levels, with the federal
government playing a supportive role.

Such emphasis at the nonfederal level should not be equated automatically with the engagement of grass-roots and community personnel. Although the rhetoric of community engagement builds on that of
the 1960s and of the family support movement, some service integration
efforts still fail to involve those whose input would be most beneficial—

namely, families and communities. Indeed, because of the increasing complexity and bureaucratization of the issues addressed via service integration efforts, the engagement of families and community members unfamiliar with the terms, processes, and stipulations is a challenge. Fortunately, to counterbalance this, grass-roots organizations focusing on community empowerment and mobilization—though not necessarily on service integration—are flourishing.

Changes in Focus

The third major difference between current and historic service integration efforts is the emphasis on a more categorical and client-based approach to the issues (Kahn and Kamerman 1992). Rather than beginning with the entire human service system as the unit of intervention, 1990s efforts are considerably more modest in the scope of services, usually emanating from one domain or discipline. Such strategies typically use the single domain as the hub from which many sectors of integration radiate. Moreover, they do not attempt change at all levels or in all functions (such as funding, planning, and accountability) at the same time. They are more realistic about the complexities and the pace of change.

Recalling an analysis of the SITO interventions, Yessian (1991) quotes from the final evaluation report of the Community Life Association (CLA) SITO Project, noting, "It can be argued that any system has only limited toleration of innovation; yet CLA sought innovation across the entire human service system, from top to bottom. But it is a fair—though unanswered—question to ask whether more modest, clearly focused goals of reform at fewer points in the human service system would have had some greater results" (p. A-5). Most current service integration strategies (except those with large funding from foundations or the federal government) seem to be addressing this question and accepting Edelman and Radin's (1991a) admonition for more humble and modest efforts.

Such a focus has resulted in stressing client-based efforts over systemic efforts (though, to be certain, systemic reform abounds in the literature and is making its way into practice). A client-based focus—centering on Agranoff and Pattakos's (1979) first dimension—suggests that agencies recognize the need to treat clients holistically and focus on the family rather than viewing single members in isolation. "Looking at fields and domains, we also note a . . . quite significant characteristic of the recent and current developments: an explicit focus on child and family services rather than social services generally, and an emphasis on the family unit (parents and children) as the client or target" (Kahn and Kamerman 1992, p. 33).

Changes in Strategies

Another major distinction between current and former efforts is the focus on standards and accountability. Capoccia (1973) notes that a key provision of the Allied Services Act established the ability to waive standards of service. Predicated on the assumption that such waivers promote flexibility, the proposed act would have sanctioned shifting eligibility requirements and levels of service. But, as Capoccia observes, if standards mark only the minimal requirements for effective service delivery, elimination of such service protections could be injurious to clients, either denying them services individually or eliminating the provision of some services collectively. Correcting this approach to waivers, current service integration efforts, more appropriately, call not for service waivers but for procedural waivers that, in contrast, act as incentives for broadening eligibility requirements and encouraging interservice agreements. Summing up the differences in approach, Capoccia notes in his criticism of the Allied Services Act, "In most cases, the interest of consumers of services would be better promoted and protected by an Allied Services effort which stimulates the development of such flexible standards rather than by the abandonment of existing ones" (p. 249). Capoccia would no doubt be pleased to see the 1990s round of service integration efforts.

A renewed vision of standards and waivers is not the only strategy that differentiates 1990s efforts from past initiatives. More than at any time in our history, service integration efforts are addressing outcome accountability. Yessian (1991) states that "in retrospect, SI projects of the 1970s and to a lesser extent the 1980s probably gave too much attention to comprehensive planning and not enough to measuring results" (p. 9). Present-day efforts, in accord with their counterparts in education in particular, are grappling with inventive approaches to measuring client outcomes as well as cost-benefit outcomes. The rationales for such an interest in outcome accountability are many. For example, Gardner (1991a) suggests that "the shift in perspective that can breathe new life into a movement toward decategorization is a genuine valuation of people and a recognition of what we all lose when so many of our children and families fail" (p. 16). He notes that measures of child, family, and community well-being offer the basis on which to argue for decategorization. Other rationales for outcome accountability are predicated on the knowledge that over time, such information will be amalgamated to provide a data base that will contribute to our understanding of human service delivery and the efficacy of these reforms.

In summary, several general points need to be made about these changes. First, they spell out a markedly different approach to service integration than has been tried before. Indeed, on all the key dimensions—attitudes, locus, focus, and strategies—1990s efforts are different from their predecessors. Second, these differences are not the result of a systematic plan and are not characteristic of service integration alone. Rather, they reflect the current ideological zeitgeist. Calls for accountability ring throughout the human services; the need to forge links across sectors and to energize localities has been the clarion call of presidential administrations under a variety of terms ("public-private partnerships," "a thousand points of light"). In human services, greater emphasis is being placed at the point of first contact with clients, and a multigenerational, family-centered strategy is being pursued. Thus, current service integration efforts must be seen not only as different from their predecessors but as barometers of their era and context.

Third, simply because they are different does not ensure that the current service integration efforts will be any easier to implement than their predecessors or that we are any wiser about implementation than our forebears. The challenges posed by the outcome orientation alone are herculean. Despite improved technology and data systems, the ethical and methodological considerations such an effort poses make it likely to flounder without sustained support. The involvement of frontline workers and families, as proposed in the 1990s strategies, demands skills for which the majority of the workers have never been trained. The need for reforming preservice training is ubiquitous, as is the need for peer support among collaborators.

But without mechanisms to address the needs of the 1990s, service integration is likely to go the way of its predecessors. We need to acknowledge that as a product of its context, and functioning with minimal supports, service integration of the 1990s is highly vulnerable. Add to it worsening social conditions and projected alterations in human service and education needs (predicted by Hodgkinson [1989], among others), and the picture becomes more clouded. If service integration of the 1990s is constructed as a mere reflection of the current context, will it be sufficiently deft, agile, and foresightful to meet the new demands of the next century? If it is undersupported to meet current need, how can it thrive to accommodate future needs?

The Future of Service Integration

At this important juncture, service integration of the 1990s needs critical attention if it is to remain fresh and vibrant and if the nation is to capitalize on the current momentum. Though possessing the potential to be an effective agent of change, service integration as it is presently construed and supported is underutilized as a tool of social reform. To bolster recent efforts and simultaneously prepare for the future, those working on service integration need to focus on six areas: (1) constructing clear definitions, goals, and principles, (2) moving the service integration agenda, (3) formulating implementation supports, (4) developing collective accountability, (5) creating new knowledge, and (6) elaborating legislative and procedural strategies that support service integration.

Constructing Definitions, Goals, and Principles

Having reviewed the history of various service integration efforts, we can easily see why confusion grows as programs proliferate. Service integration is a bit like Shah's (1971) elephant: each curious citizen who touches a part of it comes to a unique misguided conclusion about the whole. How can one thing—no matter how wondrous—feel like a hosepipe (the trunk), a fan (the ear), a pillar (the leg), and a throne (the back) at the same time?

Service integration, lacking an agreed-upon definition, does look different to each beholder. Information about it (strategies, outcomes) differs depending on the definition used. And though seemingly clear to those who "touch" it, service integration remains a highly enigmatic and divisive issue—and consequently is bereft of a constituency.

This need not be the case. The literature contains many thoughtful definitions of service integration that distinguish its domains from one another and relate each to the whole. As indicated earlier, we favor— because of its thoroughness—the definition offered by Agranoff and Pattakos (1979), which enables one to conceptualize the range of possibilities embraced by service integration, to see the parts *and* the whole. Whether this definition is the most appropriate or not, the field needs to come to some consensus on what service integration is and what constitutes its functional dimensions.

Such a definition should not be driven solely by strategies, as much of the past literature has tended to favor. For instance, the noted Gans and Horton study (1975) framed its recommendations on can-do strategies. Though they were appropriate to that era, 1990s service integration demands an approach that transcends strategies and focuses on a vision of what these efforts should both entail and accomplish. For example, we must seriously reconsider the viability of a service integration strategy that does not embrace the expansion of citizens' social and economic opportunities, which help to reduce the need for services.

Beyond delineating the scope of service integration, we must give attention to its goals and raison d'être. We need to envision more broadly and grapple more inventively with philosophical and moral questions concerning the appropriate role and function of service integration efforts in our society. What do we really expect service integration to accomplish? Do—and should—our expectations differ by dimension? Who should define the purposes? Is the emphasis on accessibility, continuity, and efficiency enunciated nearly two decades ago still sufficient today? What is our moral and social obligation to ensure quality within the service integration effort? Moreover, we need to understand service integration within the compendium of strategies for change. Is service integration one of many tools of social reform? Is it the primary tool of institutional reform? What is its role in a society that prizes autonomy and privacy in its individual and institutional ethos? This press for greater cogency of intention is a prerequisite for moving service integration from being purely a strategy to being a more visionary and durable endeavor.

Beyond the definition and goals, principles of service integration need to be codified. Without being prescriptive, such principles should draw from both literature and practice the fundamental truths that we know undergird service integration. Serving as practical guidelines for reformers, these principles should not reflect romanticized beliefs but should amalgamate viable practices that work in a form that supports the definition and goals and is functional for the field.

To achieve these aims, an inclusive forum for their deliberation must be instituted. Such a forum should be sustained over time, should have access to leading scholars and workers in the field, and should create a consensual process for accomplishing this work. Without organizational, intellectual, and practical glue, these efforts will remain isolated projects, denying the field its rightful inheritance. A consolidated effort to enunciate a definition, goals, and principles should become the foundation upon which future service integration is built.

Any effort to delineate more precisely the definitions, goals, and principles of service integration must take into account that such efforts, to date, have been built around terminology and theories essential for scholars and practitioners who have dealt with difficult technical and organizational issues. In creating a technical nomenclature, however, service integration advocates have rendered the message (and hence the movement) inaccessible to those less familiar with the field. Indeed, the constructs associated with service integration remain remote from precisely those who need to understand them best—policy makers, human service decision makers, corporate leaders, and the public at large—thereby denying the movement a powerful constituency of support.

It could be argued that service integration is akin to management by objective or total quality management; it is a means, a mechanism internal to organizational functioning that permits the organization to meet its goals more effectively. As such, it does not need to be accessible to policy or public audiences, who are generally preoccupied with ends or results. Another perspective suggests that service integration represents more than an internal strategy; it is a philosophy or a set of attitudes not only worthy of promulgation, but in need of it. This perspective suggests that service integration is so fundamental a precept that it must be understood as more than an operational strategy—it is a permeating philosophy that guides organizational means and ends. Because it is a fundamental orientation of the organization, service integration must be well understood by those both inside and outside the organization.

To date, the field of service integration not only lacks clarity of definition, goals, and principles, but it lacks a crisp language through which they may be expressed in ways that are accessible to the public and to policymakers. To advance, the field needs to become concerned with the language it uses to convey its intent; its nomenclature must be simplified and streamlined.

But accessible language, while necessary, is not the only strategy needed to move the service integration agenda. Legislators, concerned with budget constraints, continue to press for evidence of program success, notably in the form of outcome accountability. Does the program work? Does the investment of dollars make a difference? The service integration field needs to examine its capacity to deal with such questions of efficacy and to identify and remove inhibitors to clear evidence of positive outcomes. Helping decision makers understand that regulatory flexibility is a likely precursor to outcome attainment is imperative. Equally imperative is setting the policy wheels in motion to provide supports that will enable service integration work to thrive. For example, public governmental endorsement of service integration as a federal priority could accelerate support within and outside government and help build the necessary constituency for service integration.

In addition to engaging government, the field of service integration needs to look to the corporate sector for support. The corporate world's knowledge of organizational efficiency, its outcome orientation, its ability to package products and messages effectively, and its agility in moving its own policy agenda all provide domains of learning for the service integration field.

Moving to action is a complex task that involves more than commandeering media attention, alluring legislators, and engaging business and industry. It demands a paradigm shift in the way these parties conceive appropriate means and ends of human services. Such a shift will not come easily and it will not occur until the service integration message is backed by empirical data that attest to its effectiveness. As such, any shift in thinking will not occur independent of the other five recommendations made herein. It will only occur as part of a mind-set that reprioritizes human services and education and legitimates invention.

Formulating Implementation Supports

Training. Even with clear goals and values and a commitment to action, service integration of the 1990s will need to offer some tangible implementation supports—the skills and resources necessary to carry out integration reforms—to those working in the field. Perhaps the most pressing need is for workers who both understand service integration strategies and can put them into operation. Gardner (1991a) sums up the sentiment: "Running good pilot projects won't change the system if the universities keep teaching it wrong" (p. 18). To be sure, universities and other human service training institutions, locked into their disciplinary categories, do little to model or teach collaborative strategies to future leaders. Responsive observation, negotiation, and management skills need to be accompanied by a more holistic orientation to families and communities and a broader conception of the worker's role. Training programs must provide opportunities for human service workers to get experience in finance, public relations, and advocacy. Indeed, efforts are under way in the states of California and Washington to change curriculum and training methods so as to render preprofessional training programs more sensitive to service integration needs.

Beyond curricular modifications, establishing the goals and principles discussed above would help codify the content and process of training across disciplines. Such standards would specify the principles, dimensions, and components of collaborative work that could be incorporated into revamped pedagogy. In the absence of the consensus such standards represent, there is little rationale to alter instruction. Incentives are needed that would hasten the modification of curriculum to include information on linkages, on cross-agency planning and budgeting, on purchase-of-service agreements, on the benefits and liabilities of collocation, and on the need for relationship building.

Gardner's comments foist blame on the universities, which certainly are not exempt from criticism. But the need for retraining pervades all the places where human service professionals are socialized to, prepared for, and conduct their work. For example, there is a need for employers to provide ample time for workers to express their concerns and fears, and to examine their own values regarding human service delivery in general and service integration in particular. There is a need for site-based, in-service training for frontline workers regarding service integration and community empowerment strategies. Training must be envisioned as more than a university responsibility and more than a set of didactic inputs.

Technical assistance. Increases in the capacity for integration will not emerge overnight. A national technical assistance network, where thoughtful practitioners can provide and partake in skill building and practice refinement, needs nurturance. Mechanisms for sharing information across and among state and local projects must be developed and supported. Plans to train frontline personnel for leadership positions warrant serious attention.

Funding. Finally, there is a need for long-term fiscal support for service integration that allows it the opportunity for invention and experimentation. Though common in business and industry, where risk-taking and occasional failure are recognized as integral components in the process of advancement, experimentation in service integration is repressed by the fear of instant condemnation if objectives are not fully realized. To expect perfect performance from inventors misplaces the emphasis and intent. The art of service integration is still developing; it needs the space and support to make mistakes as well as the security to try again.

Developing Collective Accountability

Perhaps the most perplexing component of the service integration puzzle concerns outcome. We need to reach agreement on what constitutes positive outcomes, how to measure outcomes, and how to attribute responsibility for outcomes.

To date, there is general acknowledgment that service integration efforts need to be far more responsive to child and family outcomes as indices of success. Such an orientation, though appropriate in whatever domain of focus—client-centered, program-centered, policy-centered, or organizationally centered—is far more pronounced in efforts that focus on the first and second domains. For the third and fourth domains, the viability of these as the sole outcome measures warrants examination. It is conceivable that critical policy-centered efforts might not yield enhanced child and family outcomes, but might meet other legitimate and productive social goals (such as the elimination of service duplication and the promotion of cost-effectiveness in worker preparation and in-service training). Standards of accountability, then, need to be consensually developed for each domain, prescribing the conditions under which such standards would pertain.

Ascertaining the process and measures for collective accountability presents another challenge for those concerned about the efficacy of service integration. Contrary to our current system of accountability, which imposes numerous mechanisms for within-system accountability, few service integration projects have grappled with distributing accountability between (or among) systems. Yet, if service integration is successful as a process, agencies will share goals, be engaged in serving the same client, support the same program, and advocate the same policies. How then is outcome accounted for across the entire unit, and to whom is its accomplishment or failure attributed? Within the evaluation literature, work is being done on new approaches to evaluation, and new paradigms are being created. Applying these to service integration and to other major systemic reforms will be a formidable task, though not impossible. With resources and scholarly minds devoted to this issue, inroads will be made. An evaluation forum specifically related to service integration should be established so that leading methodologists and practitioners can come together to create a service integration evaluation strategy that meets the demands already being made of it.

Creating New Knowledge

Within our society, foundations have often supported wise and controlled experimentation. Such has been the case in service integration in the 1990s, and it is from these experiments that service integration will move forward. But investment from foundations should not preclude government investment in generating knowledge. To the contrary, a comprehensive analysis of service integration should be launched combining public- and private-sector support.

Gnawing questions about the value of integrated services have pervaded the literature of the last twenty years, with each investigator lamenting the lack of definitive answers. Until a well-designed, well-implemented national study of service integration using clearly delineated definitions, goals, and principles is undertaken, such questions will never cease to be posed.

A longitudinal research and demonstration study should form the basis for such an effort. The study should begin in years one and two by clarifying definitions, goals, and principles, as outlined above. Simultaneously, it should identify target communities, and within the target communities training efforts that incorporate the pedagogical alterations discussed above should be launched. In some cases, such training will not require renegotiation of roles and functions across institutions. In other cases, those negotiations should be undertaken as the necessary prelude to training reform. But under no circumstance should training be delayed until such reforms are accomplished. The goal is to have trained service integration specialists who will be able to staff the demonstration projects. In years three and four, a bilevel, state-local service integration system would be established by identifying service capacities and needs, by circumscribing goals, and by linking explicit strategies to the selected domains.

Simultaneously with start-up, technical assistance should be provided to the efforts and a national network formed. An evaluation plan, developed in years one and two, would be tailored to site plans in year three and launched with the main service integration activities in year four. Process data would be collected, as would outcome data over a period of four years. The data would be analyzed and findings presented in year nine, with year ten reserved for dissemination and "scaling up," should the results of this controlled experiment suggest that it is warranted. Such a plan could be tailored to match the timelines of emerging initiatives in the public and private sectors and could serve as a source of companion data.

Incorporating a shared, multidomain conceptualization of service integration, specific domain-targeted strategies and similarly targeted evaluations of process and outcomes, structured flexibility at the local level, and durational support, such a longitudinal effort promises to bring a new level of understanding to the implementation of service integration. Without such a systematized approach, service integration efforts in the 1990s are likely to falter like many of their predecessors. Those that are well supported will have a longer life; less well supported efforts will inch along to their eventual demise, having rendered little more than a short-term infusion of energy. Tomorrow's social problems deserve the carefully considered application of one of today's most promising social strategies.

Elaborating Legislative and Procedural Strategies

Beyond the need for new knowledge, there must be mechanisms to receive such knowledge and promising strategies to act upon it. Legislation should encourage—rather than discourage—comprehensive state planning mechanisms or bodies that transcend funding categories. Such planning mechanisms, once established, should specify clear outcomes and the means and timelines for their evaluation. Further, legislation should allow governors to renegotiate federal matching rates, redeploy resources, and consolidate categorical programs at the state level. A permissive legislative strategy of this sort would enable states to plan service delivery and accountability tailored to specific state needs.

The question of accountability has resurfaced throughout this analysis, but little attention has been given to who will actually set the standards against which performance will be measured. Greater engagement of the consumers of services in the standard-setting process, via policy councils (as in Head Start), resident management committees, or local consumer councils, should be considered. Such engagement can create more knowledgeable consumers who will make the system more responsive to their needs.

Inequities in access to services, caused by somewhat arbitrary eligibility cut-offs, have long plagued service providers. Rather than a bevy of policies that determine access by a specific income threshold, thereby declaring individuals either "in" or "out," more malleable access patterns, such as those employing a sliding scale, should be considered.

Finally, there is a need to reconsider the scheduling of program reauthorizations so that similar programs come up for reconsideration simultaneously. For example, reauthorization of the special education legislation should coincide with that of the education-related Hawkins-Stafford Amendment of 1988 so that inventive linkages can be built into both pieces of legislation rather than into only one. Similarly, new legislation should be required to include service impact statements that would specify how the legislation would interact with existing efforts. Fewer "whereas's" and more "how linked's" in the legislative language would fortify the likelihood of new efforts being tied effectively to existing policies and programs.

Conclusion

Throughout this book, considerable stress has been placed on moving beyond convention, on breaking the mold, on daring to invent and reinvent. Service integration demands such approaches. It can no longer be conceived, implemented, or evaluated according to prior notions. It must be re-envisioned. Indeed, service integration must be thought of as a philosophy, as a component of many disciplines, and as a strategy.

Service integration as a philosophy. More than discrete activities, service integration must be understood as a fundamental approach to service delivery, one that is different in orientation and that stems from a different philosophy. It demands an attitudinal conversion from competition to collaboration, from exclusion to inclusion, from involvement to empowerment, and from restricted to holistic approaches to human services.

Service integration as a component of many disciplines. The theoretical perspectives that undergird service integration have been extruded from numerous disciplines, as we have seen. Yet although initially drawn from disparate sources, the body of knowledge that has been amalgamated is sufficiently unique so as to constitute a different domain of inquiry, replete with its own theories, literature, and approaches.

However robust, this domain of inquiry has to date remained comparatively remote from the primary disciplines that spawned it. Service integration as a body of knowledge and practical skills has not returned to its roots to inform mainstream disciplines; it has not been routinely incorporated into professional preparation programs in social work, education, human services, or medicine. But as a unique and relevant domain of inquiry, it can help refuel conventional disciplines theoretically and practically. Indeed, service integration should become a component of health, social service, community development, social work, teacher preparation, and administrator training, at a minimum. As such, service integration needs to recognize itself as a valid and essential component of all human service professions.

Service integration as a strategy. Historically, service integration has been viewed as a strategy. Such an orientation has limited the ability of service integration efforts to take root and thus provides the rationale for the above two reconceptualizations. This does not mean, however, that service integration should not be considered a strategy as well. Indeed, service integration is grounded in the reality of a dysfunctional system, a system that is every day failing the people it was developed to serve and the society at large. Time and lives do not permit a theoretical focus that promises only to delay change. Service integration must remain, in part, strategy-driven, but the strategies must be more finely honed. They must match specific and differentiated goals, with a clear focus on outcomes. Strategies must be constructed with knowledge of their limitations and their demands, and with knowledge of their interactive effects.

When all is said and done, service integration in its present form remains enigmatic. As products of their contexts, without consensus of definitions, goals, or principles, projects are highly idiosyncratic and vulnerable to political and ideological shifts. Possessing promise, but lacking durability, service integration efforts are prime candidates for reconceptualization and reevaluation. Such an investment of energies must be undertaken comprehensively: we must not tinker at the edges on a project-by-project basis but must approach the challenges of developing a reframed vision and philosophy of service integration with vigor and optimism. Little would do more to honor the generations of service integrators who have given of themselves without confirmed knowledge of the outcome of their work, or to advance the state of human service delivery in our nation.

References

Abernathy, M. G. 1984. Domestic civil rights. In M. G. Abernathy, D. M. Hill, and P. Williams (eds.), *The Carter years: The president and policy making*, pp. 106–22. London: Frances Pinter.

Addams, J. [1910] 1972. *The spirit of youth and the city streets.* Urbana: University of Illinois Press.

Agranoff, R. A. 1974. Human services administration: Service delivery, service integration and training. In T. J. Mikulecky (ed.), *Human services integration.* Washington, D.C.: American Society for Public Administration.

————. 1977. Services integration. In W. Anderson, M. Murphy, and B. Friedan (eds.), *Managing human services.* Washington, D.C.: International City Management Association.

————. 1986. *Intergovernmental management: Human services problem-solving in six metropolitan areas.* Albany, N.Y.: State University of New York Press.

————. 1988. Structuring of human services in local government: Management versus reorganization. *New England Journal of Human Services* 8:10–18.

————. 1991. Human services integration: Past and present challenges in public administration. *Public Administration Review* 51 (6): 533–42.

Agranoff, R. A., and A. N. Pattakos. 1979. Dimensions of services integration: Service delivery, program linkages, policy management, organizational structure. Human Services Monograph Series, 13. Washington, D.C.: U.S. Department of Health, Education and Welfare, Project SHARE.

————. 1989. Management of human services in local governments: A national survey. *State and Local Government Review* 21:74–83.

Alford, R. 1975. *Health care politics*. Chicago: University of Chicago Press.

Allington, R. L., and P. Johnston. 1989. Coordination, collaboration and consistency: The redesign of compensatory and special education interventions. In R. E. Slavin, N. L. Karweit, and N. A. Madden (eds.), *Effective programs for students at risk*, pp. 320–354. Boston: Allyn and Bacon.

Altman, D. 1991. The challenges of service integration for children and families. In L. B. Schorr, D. Both, and C. Copple (eds.), *Effective services for young children: Report of a workshop*, pp. 74–79. Washington, D.C.: National Academy Press.

Altshuler, A. 1970. *Community control*. Indianapolis: Pegasus.

American Public Welfare Association. 1976. *Integrated social services: A comparison between an integrated and a categorical social service system*. Washington, D.C.: Author.

Anderson, W. 1960. *Intergovernmental relations in review*. Minneapolis: University of Minnesota Press.

Argyris, C. 1957. *Personality and organization*. New York: Harper and Row.

Austin, D. M. 1982. Human services. In H. Orlans (ed.), *Human services coordination: A panel report and accompanying papers*, pp. 1–21. New York: Pica Press.

Axinn, J., and H. Levin. 1975. *Social welfare: A history of the American response to need*. New York: Dodd Mead.

Banfield, E. 1971. Revenue sharing in theory and practice. *Public Interest* 23:33–44.

Barfield, C. E. 1981. *Rethinking federalism: Block grants and federal, state, and local responsibilities.* Washington, D.C.: American Enterprise Institute.

Barnard, C. 1938. *The functions of the executive.* Cambridge, Mass.: Harvard University Press.

Bennis, W. 1966. *Changing organizations.* New York: McGraw-Hill.

Blank, M., and J. Lombardi. 1992. *Towards improved services for children and families: Forging new relationships through collaboration.* Washington, D.C.: Institute for Educational Leadership.

Blum, B. B. 1982. Coordinated service: The state experience. In H. Orlans (ed.), *Human services coordination: A panel report and accompanying papers,* pp. 78–95. New York: Pica Press.

Bourne, P. G. 1974. Human resources: A new approach to the dilemmas of community psychiatry. *American Journal of Psychiatry, 131* (6): 666–69.

Bowers, G. E., and M. R. Bowers. 1977. Cultivating client information systems. Human Services Monograph Series, 5. Washington, D.C.: U.S. Department of Health, Education and Welfare, Project SHARE.

Brager, G., and S. Holloway. 1978. *Changing human service organizations: Politics and practice.* New York: Free Press.

Bremner, R. H. 1970. *Children and youth in America: A documentary history.* Vol. 2, pts. 1–6. Cambridge, Mass.: Harvard University Press.

Brewer, G. D., and J. S. Kakalik. 1979. *Handicapped children: Strategies for improving services.* New York: McGraw-Hill.

Briar, S. 1982. Services integration and coordination in the West: The Washington State experience. In H. Orlans (ed.), *Human services coordination,* pp. 115–24. New York: Pica Press.

Brooks, M. 1971. *Social planning and city planning.* Chicago: American Society of Planning Officials.

Brueckner, W. H. 1963. *Human problems in the core city: Current thinking on the role of the settlement.* Unpublished proceedings of a conference, The Mental Health Role of the Settlement and Community Centers, October 23–25, Swampscott, Mass.

Bruner, C. 1989a. State innovations in children and family services collaboration and financing. In C. L. Romig (ed.), *Family policy: Recommendations for state action,* pp. 163–72. Washington, D.C.: National Conference of State Legislators.

References

————. 1989b. *Is change from above possible? State-level strategies for supporting street-level services.* Des Moines, Iowa: Child and Family Policy Center.

————. 1991. *Thinking collaboratively.* Washington, D.C.: Education and Human Services Consortium.

Bruner, C., and D. Flintrop. 1991. *Developing comprehensive family centered child welfare systems: Emerging state strategies.* Des Moines, Iowa: Child and Family Policy Center.

Bush, M. 1988. *Families in distress.* Berkeley and Los Angeles: University of California Press.

Cahan, E. 1989. *Past caring.* New York: National Center for Children in Poverty, School of Public Health, Columbia University.

Capoccia, V. A. 1973. Social welfare planning and the New Federalism: The Allied Services Act. *Journal of the American Institute of Planners,* July:244–53.

Carlucci, F. 1974. *Testimony before the Committee on Education and Labor of the U.S. House of Representatives.* July 10.

Center for the Future of Children. 1992. *The future of children: School-linked services.* Los Altos, Calif.: David and Lucile Packard Foundation.

Chapel Hill Training Outreach Project. 1988. *Transitions from pre-school to kindergarten.* Chapel Hill, N.C.: Author.

Chi, K. S. 1987. What has happened to the comprehensive human services agency? *New England Journal of Human Services* 7:25.

Cohen, N. 1958. *Social work in the American tradition.* New York: Dryden.

Community Life Association. 1974. *Hartford SITO project documentation: Pooled funding as a method of achieving services integration: The use of case management and purchase of service contracts in the Community Life Association.* Unpublished report.

Comprehensive Human Services Planning and Delivery. N.d. Unpublished manuscript of the Department of Health, Education and Welfare. New York: Columbia University School of Social Work, National Center for Children in Poverty, National Center for Service Integration Clearinghouse.

Conlan, T. 1988. *New federalism: Intergovernmental reform from Nixon to Reagan.* Washington, D.C.: Brookings Institution.

Copeland W. C., and I. A. Iversen. 1981. Refinancing and reorganizing human services: Interagency net budgeting and other fiscal incentives. Human Services Monograph Series, 20. Washington, D.C.: U.S. Department of Health and Human Services, Project SHARE.

Coser, L. A., and O. N. Larsen (eds.). 1976. *The uses of controversy in sociology.* New York: Free Press.

Cotter, B. 1981. Planning and implementing social service information systems: A guide for management and users. Human Services Monograph Series, 25. Washington, D.C.: U.S. Department of Health and Human Services, Project SHARE.

Council of State Governments. 1974. *Human Services Integration: State Families in Implementation.* Lexington, Ky.: Author.

Cremin, L. 1977. *Traditions of American education.* New York: Basic Books.

Crowson, R. L., and W. Boyd. 1992. *Coordinated services for children: Designing arks for storms and seas unknown.* Philadelphia: National Center on Education in the Inner Cities.

CSR. 1986. *Report on progress and status of Services Integration Pilot Projects: First year planning phase.* Washington, D.C.: Author.

Curtis, W. R. 1976. *The development of agency coordination and service integration: The area-based matrix organization.* Boston: Social Matrix.

———. 1981. Managing human services with less: New strategies for local leaders. Human Services Monograph Series, 26. Washington, D.C.: U.S. Department of Health and Human Services, Project SHARE.

Dempsey, J. T. 1982. Coordination of human services for the 1980s. In H. Orlans (ed.), *Human services coordination: A panel report and accompanying papers,* pp. 96–114. New York: Pica Press.

Division of State Planning and Community Affairs. 1974. *Human services planning, financing and delivery in Virginia.* Vol. 2, *Services integration techniques transferable to other states.* Richmond, Va.: Author.

Edelman, P. B., and B. A. Radin. 1991a. *Serving children and families effectively: How can the past help chart the future?* Washington, D.C.: Education and Human Services Consortium.

———. 1991b. Effective services for children and families: Lessons from the past and strategies for the future. In L. B. Schorr, D. Both, and C. Copple (eds.), *Effective services for young children: Report of a workshop,* pp. 48–64. Washington, D.C.: National Academy Press.

Edgar, E., and M. Maddox. 1983. The cookbook model: An approach to inter-agency collaboration. In *Perspectives on interagency collaboration,* pp. 19–28. National Invitational Symposium on Interagency Collaboration, March, Denver, Colo. ERIC Document Reproduction Service No. ED 235 669.

Eisenhower, D. D. 1953. Remarks at the Governors' Conference, August 4, Seattle, Wash. *Public Papers of the Presidents.*

Elder, J. O., and P. R. Magrab. 1980. *Coordinating services to handicapped children: A handbook for interagency collaboration.* Baltimore: Paul H. Brookes.

Family Impact Seminar. 1992. *Service integration and coordination at the family/client level: Is case management the answer?* Background briefing report. Washington, D.C.: Research and Education Foundation, American Association for Marriage and Family Therapy.

Farrow, F., and T. Joe. 1992. Financing school-linked, integrated services. In *The Future of Children,* pp. 56–67. Los Altos, Calif.: Center for the Future of Children.

Feild, T., R. D'Amico, and B. Benton. 1978. *Utah unification project: Measuring the client impact of services integration.* Washington, D.C.: Urban Institute.

Fessler, J. W. 1973. The basic theoretical question: How to relate area and function. In L. Grosenick (ed.), *The administration of the new federalism: Objectives and issues,* pp. 4–11. Washington, D.C.: American Society for Public Administration.

Firestone, W. A., and D. H. Drews. 1987. *The coordination of education and social services: Implications from three programs.* Washington, D.C.: Department of Education, Office of Educational Research and Improvement. ERIC Document Reproduction Service No. ED 291 002.

Fishman, M. E., and J. V. Dolson. N.d. *The evolution of human services integration: A federal perspective.* Unpublished paper. Columbia University School of Social Work, National Center for Children in Poverty, National Center for Service Integration Clearinghouse.

Friesema, H. P. 1969. Black control of central cities: The hollow prize. *Journal of the American Institute of Planners* 35 (2): 75–79.

Gallagher, J. J., G. Harbin, D. Thomas, R. Clifford, and M. Wenger. 1988. *Major policy issues in implementing Part H-P.L. 99–457 (infants and toddlers).* Chapel Hill: University of North Carolina, Carolina Institute for Child and Family Policy.

Gans, S. P., and G. T. Horton. 1975. *Integration of human services: The state and municipal levels.* New York: Praeger.

Gardner, S. 1976. Roles for general purpose governments in human services. Human Services Monograph Series, 2. Washington, D.C.: U.S. Department of Health, Education and Welfare, Project SHARE.

———. 1991a. A commentary. In *Serving children and families effectively: How the past can help chart the future.* Washington, D.C.: Education and Human Services Consortium.

———. 1991b. *Community report cards: Making kids count.* Fullerton: California State University.

Gawthrop, L. C. 1984. *Public sector management, systems, and ethics.* Bloomington: Indiana University Press.

Gerry, M. In press. *A joint enterprise with American families to ensure student success.* Washington, D.C.: Council of Chief State School Officers.

Gilbert, N. 1970. *Clients or constituents.* San Francisco: Jossey-Bass.

Gilbert, N., and H. Specht. 1977. *Coordinating social services: An analysis of community, organizational, and staff characteristics.* New York: Praeger.

Graves, W. B. 1964. *American intergovernmental relations: Their origins, historical development, and current status.* New York: Scribner.

Grubb, W. N., and M. Lazerson. 1982. *Broken promises: How Americans fail their children.* New York: Basic Books.

Gulick, L. 1937. Notes on the theory of organization. In L. Gulick and L. Urwick (eds.), *Papers on the science of administration.* New York: Augustus Kelley.

Gulick, L., and L. Urwick (eds.). 1937. *Papers on the science of administration.* New York: Augustus Kelley.

Hagebak, B. R. 1979. Local human service delivery: The integration imperative. *Public Administration Review* 39:575–581.

Halpern, R. 1991. Supportive services for families in poverty: Dilemmas of reform. *Social Service Review* 65 (3): 343–364.

Harbin, G., and B. McNulty. 1990. Policy implementation: Perspectives on service coordination and interagency cooperation. In S. J. Meisels and J. Shonkoff (eds.), *Handbook of early childhood intervention.* New York: Cambridge University Press.

Harmon, M., and R. Mayer. 1986. *Organization theory for public administration.* Boston: Little, Brown.

Hawkins, R. R. 1977. Drink deep or waste not . . . Are there any other choices? *Public Management 59* (5): 11–13.

Hayes, C., J. Palmer, and M. Zaslow. 1990. *Who cares for America's children? Child care policy for the 1990s.* Washington, D.C.: National Academy Press.

Hearings before the Subcommittee on Intergovernmental Relations of the Senate Government Operations Committee. 1966. *Creative federalism.* 89 Cong., 2d sess., p. 267.

Helge, D. 1984. *Problems and strategies regarding regionalizing service delivery: Educational collaboratives in rural America.* February. Murray, Ky.: Murray State University, National Rural Research Project. ERIC Document Reproduction Service No. ED 242 449.

Henry, N. B. 1953. *The fifty-second yearbook of the National Society for the Study of Education.* Part 2, *The community school.* Chicago: University of Chicago Press.

Hill, D. M. 1984. Domestic policy. In M. G. Abernathy, D. M. Hill, and P. Williams (eds.), *The Carter years: The president and policy making,* pp. 13–34. London: Frances Pinter.

Himmelman, A. 1991. *Communities working collaboratively for change.* Minneapolis: Himmelman Consulting Group.

Hodgkinson, H. 1989. *The same client: The demographics of education and service delivery systems.* Washington, D.C.: Institute for Educational Leadership and Center for Demographic Policy.

Ink, D. 1973. The origins and thrusts of the new federalism. In L. Grosenick (ed.), *The administration of the new federalism: Objectives and issues,* pp. 29–33. Washington, D.C.: American Society for Public Administration.

Intagliata, J. 1981. Operationalizing a case management system: A multi-level approach. In *Case management: State of the art,* pp. 98–134. Washington, D.C.: National Conference on Social Welfare. NTIS No. PB82–155961.

Jackson, E. 1973. The present system of publicly supported day care. In D. Young and R. R. Nelson (eds.), *Public policy for day care of young children,* pp. 21–46. Lexington, Mass.: Lexington Books.

John, D. 1977. Managing the human service "system": What have we learned from services integration? Human Services Monograph Series 4. Washington, D.C.: U.S. Department of Health and Human Services, Project SHARE.

Johnson, H. W., J. A. McLaughlin, and M. Christensen. 1982. Interagency collaboration: Driving and restraining forces. *Exceptional Children* 48 (5): 395–99.

Johnson, L. B. 1966. Budget message, January 24. *Public Papers of the Presidents.*

Joint Commission on Mental Health of Children. 1969. *Crisis in child mental health: Challenge for the 1970s.* New York: Harper and Row.

Jordan, F. 1971. Model cities in perspective: A selective history. In *Model cities: A report on progress.* Special issues of the Model Cities Service Center Bulletin. Washington, D.C.: Government Printing Office.

Kagan, S. L. 1987. Home-school linkages: History's legacies and the family support movement. In S. L. Kagan, D. Powell, B. Weissbourd, and E. Zigler (eds.), *America's family support programs.* New Haven: Yale University Press.

———. 1991. *United we stand: Collaboration for child care and early education services.* New York: Teachers College Press.

Kagan, S. L., A. Rivera, N. Brigham, and S. Rosenblum. 1992. *Collaboration: Cornerstone of an early childhood system.* New Haven: Yale University, Bush Center in Child Development and Social Policy.

Kagan, S. L., A. Rivera, and F. Lamb-Parker. 1991. *Collaboration in action: Reshaping services for young children and their families.* New Haven: Yale University, Bush Center in Child Development and Social Policy.

Kahn, A., and S. Kamerman. 1992. *Integrating services integration: An overview of initiatives, issues, and possibilities.* New York: Columbia University School of Social Work, National Center for Children in Poverty.

Kaplan, Gans, and Kahn, and the Research Group. 1973. *Integration of human services in HEW: An evaluation of services integration projects.* Vol. 1. Report No. SHR-0000127. Washington, D.C.: U.S. Department of Health, Education and Welfare.

Katz, A. H., and K. Martin. 1982. *A handbook of services for the handicapped.* Westport, Conn.: Greenwood Press.

Katz, M. 1981. Education and inequality. In D. Rothman and S. Wheeler (eds.), *Social history and social policy.* New York: Academic Press.

Kettl, D. 1984. The fourth face of federalism. In D. Wright and H. White (eds.), *Federalism and intergovernmental relations.* Washington, D.C.: American Society for Public Administration.

Kimmel, W. A. 1981. Putting program evaluation in perspective for state and local government. Human Services Monograph Series, 18. Washington, D.C.: U.S. Department of Health and Human Services, Project SHARE.

Kimmich, M. 1985. *America's children: Who cares?* Washington, D.C.: Urban Institute.

Knitzer, J. 1982. *Unclaimed children: The failure of public responsibility to children and adolescents in need of mental health services.* Washington, D.C.: Children's Defense Fund.

Knitzer, J., and S. Yelton. 1990. Collaborations between child welfare and mental health. *Public Welfare* 48 (2): 24–33.

Kramer, R. 1969. *Participation of the poor.* Englewood Cliffs, N.J.: Prentice-Hall.

Kurzman, S. N.d. *Memo to Elliot Richardson regarding proposals for services integration legislation.* Unpublished document. New York: Columbia University School of Social Work, National Center for Children in Poverty, National Center for Service Integration Clearinghouse.

Kusserow, R. P. 1991. *Services integration for families and children in crisis.* Washington, D.C.: Department of Health and Human Services, Office of the Inspector General.

Levine, J. 1978. *Day care and the public schools: Profiles of five communities.* Newton, Mass.: Education Development Center.

———. 1982. The prospects and dilemmas of child care information and referral. In E. Zigler and E. Gordon (eds.), *Day care: Scientific and social policy options.* Boston: Auburn House.

Levinson, P., and I. Hutchinson. 1973. *Alternative administrative structures in state departments of human resources.* Research and Evaluation Working Paper No. 1. Atlanta: Department of Health, Education and Welfare.

Lindblom, C., and D. Cohen. 1979. *Usable knowledge: Social science and social problem solving.* New Haven: Yale University Press.

London, K. 1976. *People side of systems.* New York: McGraw-Hill.

Lowi, T. 1969. *The end of liberalism.* New York: Norton.

Lucas, W. A. 1975. *Aggregating organizational experience with services integration: Feasibility and design.* WN-9059-HEW. Santa Monica, Calif.: Rand.

Lucas, W. A., K. Heald, and M. Vogel. 1975. *The 1975 census of local services integration.* WN-9289-HEW. Santa Monica, Calif.: Rand.

Lynn, L. 1980. *The state and human services: Organizational change in a political context*. Cambridge, Mass.: MIT Press.

Lynn, L., and D. Sprague. 1972. *Memo on service integration R and D: Status Report*. April 3. Unpublished.

McGregor, D. 1960. *The human side of enterprise*. New York: McGraw-Hill.

McLaughlin, M. 1980. Evaluation and alchemy. In J. Pincus (ed.), *Educational evaluation in the public policy setting*. Santa Monica, Calif.: Rand.

Martin, P. Y., R. Chackerian, A. Imershein, and M. Frumkin. 1983. The concept of "integrated" services reconsidered. *Social Science Quarterly* 64 (4): 747–63.

Marzke, C., C. Chimerine, W. Morrill, and E. Marks. 1992. *Service integration programs in community settings*. Contract No. LC 89089001. Washington, D.C.: U.S. Department of Education and U.S. Department of Health and Human Services.

Maslow, A. 1965. *Eupsychian management*. Homewood, Ill.: Richard Irwin.

Mattessich, P., and B. Monsey. 1992. *Collaboration: What makes it work*. St. Paul, Minn.: Amherst H. Wilder Foundation.

Melaville, A., and M. Blank. 1991. *What it takes: Structuring interagency partnerships to connect children and families with comprehensive services*. Washington, D.C.: Education and Human Services Consortium.

Mittenthal, S. 1975. *Human service development programs in sixteen allied services (SITO) projects*. Wellesley, Mass.: Human Ecology Institute.

Moore, J. 1971. *Memo to Elliot Richardson on the subject of services integration project follow-up*. April 6. Unpublished.

Morgan, G. 1972. *An evaluation of the 4-C concept*. Washington, D.C.: Day Care and Child Development Council of America.

Morgan, J. 1985. *Putting the pieces together: Making interagency collaboration work. Preschool interagency council: A model*. April. Tallahassee: Florida State Department of Education. ERIC Document Reproduction Service No. ED 296 507.

Morrill, W. A. 1991a. *Collaborations that integrate services for children and families: A framework for research*. Princeton, N.J., and Washington, D.C.: Mathtech and Policy Studies Associates.

———. 1991b. *Improving outcomes for children and families at risk—Collabora-*

References

tions which integrate services: Next steps. Contract No. LC 89089001. Washington, D.C.: U.S. Department of Education and U.S. Department of Health and Human Services.

Morrill, W. A., and M. Gerry. 1990. Integrations and coordination of services for school-aged children: Toward a definition of American experience and experimentation. Washington, D.C.: Department of Health and Human Services, Office of the Assistant Secretary for Planning and Evaluation.

Morris, R., and I. Lescohier. 1978. Service integration: Real versus illusory solutions to welfare dilemmas. In R. C. Sarri and Y. Hasenfeld (eds.), *The management of human services,* pp. 23–50. New York: Columbia University Press.

Mudd, J. 1982. Coordinating services for children. In H. Orlans (ed.), *Human services coordination: A panel report and accompanying papers,* pp. 22–45. New York: Pica Press.

Nathan, R. 1975. Federalism and the shifting nature of fiscal relations: General revenue sharing and federalism. *Annals.* May.

National Academy of Public Administration. 1977. *Reorganization in Florida: How is services integration working?* Washington, D.C.: Author.

National Academy of Sciences, National Research Council, Division of Behavioral Sciences. 1972. *Report of the Panel on the Assessment of the Community Coordinated Child Care Program.* Washington, D.C.: Author.

National Conference on Social Welfare. 1981. *Case management: State of the art.* Washington, D.C.: Author. NTIS No. PB82–155961.

National League of Cities/U.S. Conference of Mayors. 1974. *A study of the roles for cities under the allied services approach of the Department of Health, Education and Welfare.* Washington, D.C.: U.S. Department of Health, Education and Welfare.

O'Connor, R., N. Albrecht, B. Cohen, and L. Newquist-Carroll. 1984. *New directions in youth services: Experiences with state-level coordination.* Washington, D.C.: U.S. Department of Justice and U.S. Department of Health and Human Services.

Office of White House Press Secretary. 1972. *Fact sheet: Allied services message.* May 18. Washington, D.C.: Author.

Olshansky, S. 1973. Some comments on the "delivery of service." *Rehabilitation Literature* 34 (7): 203–6.

Osborne, D., and T. Gaebler. 1992. *Reinventing government: How the entrepreneurial spirit is transforming the public sector*. Reading, Mass.: Addison-Wesley.

Paul, J. L., D. J. Stedman, and G. R. Neufeld (eds.). 1977. *Deinstitutionalization: Program and policy development*. Syracuse, N.Y.: Syracuse University Press.

Pincus, J. (ed.). 1980. *Educational evaluation in the public policy setting*. Santa Monica, Calif.: Rand.

Piven, F. F., and R. A. Cloward. 1982. *The new class war: Reagan's attack on the welfare state and its consequences*. New York: Pantheon.

Pontzer, K. 1989. *Progress in state early intervention program planning under the Part H infant-toddler program: Findings of an 11-state survey*. Washington, D.C.: Mental Health Law Project.

President's Commission on Mental Health. 1978. Report to the president. Washington, D.C.: Author.

Redburn, F. S. 1977. On "human services integration." *Public Administration Review* 37:264–69.

Reese, W. J. 1978. Between home and school: Organized parents, clubwomen, and urban education in the Progressive Era. *School Review*, November:3–28.

Rein, M. 1970. *Social policy: Issues of choice and change*. New York: Random House.

Research Group. 1973. *Comparative analysis of three research strategies directed toward multi-governmental provision of public services*. Atlanta: Author.

Research Group, and Kaplan, Gans, and Kahn. 1972a. *Human resource services in the states: An analysis of state human resource agencies and the Allied Services Act of 1972*. Washington, D.C.: Department of Health, Education and Welfare, Social and Rehabilitative Services.

————.1972b. *Integration of human services in HEW: An evaluation of services integration projects*. Washington, D.C.: Department of Health, Education and Welfare, Social and Rehabilitative Services.

Resnick, H., and R. Patti. 1980. *Change from within: Humanizing social welfare organizations*. Philadelphia: Temple University Press.

Richardson, E. L. 1972. *Responsibility and Responsiveness*. DHEW Publication No. OS 72–19. Washington, D.C.: Department of Health, Education and Welfare.

————. 1976. *The creative balance: Government, politics, and the individual in America's third century.* New York: Holt, Rinehart and Winston.

Rogers, C., and F. Farrow. 1983. *Effective state strategies to promote interagency collaboration.* October. Washington, D.C.: Center for the Study of Social Policy. ERIC Document Reproduction Service No. ED 245 467.

Ross, H. 1980. *Proceedings of the Conference on the Evaluation of Case Management Programs.* Los Angeles: Volunteers for Services to Older Persons.

Rothman, D. 1971. *The discovery of the asylum: Social order and disorder in the new republic.* Boston: Little, Brown.

Sampson, B. C. 1971. *Services integration. Part 3: An overview.* Washington, D.C.: Abt Associates.

Schenet, M. A. 1982. *State education agency coordination efforts.* September. Washington, D.C.: National Institute of Education. ERIC Document Reproduction Service No. 225 235.

Schlenger, W. E., et al. 1990. *Final report: The CASSP initial cohort study.* Vol. 1: *Cross-site findings.* Durham, N.C.: Research Triangle Institute.

Schmidt, R., J. Scanlon, and J. Bell. 1979. Evaluability assessment: Making public programs work better. *Human Services Monograph Series,* 14. Washington, D.C.: U.S. Department of Health, Education and Welfare, Project SHARE.

Schorr, L. 1989. Early interventions to reduce intergenerational disadvantage: The new policy context. *Teachers College Record* 90 (3):362–74.

Schwartz, S. R., H. H. Goldman, and S. Churgin. 1982. Case management for the chronic mentally ill: Models and dimensions. *Hospital and Community Psychiatry* 33:1006–9.

Seeley, D. 1981. *Education through partnership: Mediating structures and education.* Cambridge, Mass.: Ballinger.

Shah, I. 1971. *The Sufis.* New York: Anchor Books.

Silverman, D. 1970. *Theory of organizations.* New York: Basic Books.

Simon, H. A. 1976. *Administrative behavior: A study of decision-making processes in administrative organizations.* 3d, rev. ed.. New York: Free Press.

Skarnulis, E. R. 1981. Case management functions within the context of a comprehensive service system: Where do they fit? In *Case management: State of the* art, pp. 24–46. Washington, D.C.: National Conference on Social Welfare. NTIS No. PB82–155961.

Sloan, A. P. 1964. *My years with General Motors.* New York: Doubleday.

Snider, C. F. 1937. Country and township government in 1935–1936. *American Political Science Review* 31:909.

Solarz, A. 1973. *1975–1979 Long Range Plan for Service Integration.* Unpublished document. New York: Columbia University School of Social Work, National Center for Children in Poverty, National Center for Service Integration Clearinghouse.

Soler, M., and C. Shauffer. 1990. Fighting fragmentation: Coordination of services for children and families. *Nebraska Law Review* 69 (2):278–97.

Sprague, D. 1972. *The Allied Services Act: An innovative and integrative approach to human service.* November 27. Williamsburg, Va. Unpublished speech.

State Reorganization Commission. 1989. *Services integration pilot projects: An evaluative report from Arizona, Florida, Maine, Oklahoma, South Carolina.* Columbia, S.C.: Author.

Stein, T. J. 1981. Macro and micro level issues in case management. In *Case management: State of the art,* pp. 72–97. Washington, D.C.: National Conference on Social Welfare. NTIS No. PB82–155961.

Stein, T. J., E. D. Gambrill, and K. T. Wiltse. 1977. Dividing case management in foster family cases. *Child Welfare* 56 (5):321–31.

Steiner, G. Y. 1976. *The children's cause.* Washington, D.C.: Brookings Institution.

Sundquist, J. L. 1969. *Making federalism work.* Washington, D.C.: Brookings Institution.

Tank, R. M. 1980. Young children, families and society in America since the 1820s: The evolution of health, education and child care programs for preschool children. Ph.D. diss., University of Michigan, Ann Arbor. University Microfilms International, No. 8106233.

Test, M. 1979. Continuity of care in community treatment. In L. Stein (ed.), *Community support systems for the long-term patient.* San Francisco: Jossey-Bass.

Theroux, P. 1981. Amazing Grace. *Washington Post Magazine,* October 18:34–35.

Toch, H., and J. D. Grant. 1982. *Reforming human services: Change through participation.* Beverly Hills, Calif.: Sage.

References

Tropman, J. 1971. Community welfare councils. In *Encyclopedia of Social Work*. New York: National Association of Social Workers.

Twiname, J. 1971a. *Feeder bill: Introduction*. HEW Memo, 4–23–1971. Unpublished.

———. 1971b. *Feeder bill development*. HEW Memo, 4–30–1971. Unpublished.

U.S. Department of Health and Human Services. 1983. *A review of the conceptual foundation and current status of service integration*. Washington, D.C.: Department of Health and Human Services, Office of Human Development Services, Office of Program Development.

———. 1992. *21st century communities: Concept paper*. Unpublished document.

U.S. Department of Health, Education and Welfare. 1972. *Report of the Task Force on Administrative and Organizational Constraints to Services Integration*. Washington, D.C.: Author.

———. 1974. *Fact Sheet: Allied Services Act of 1974*. January. Washington, D.C.: Author.

———. 1975a. *HEW capacity building (federal, state, and local)*. Washington, D.C.: Author.

———. 1975b. *Fact Sheet: Allied Services Act of 1975*. October. Washington, D.C.: Author.

———. 1976. *Integration of human services in HEW: An evaluation of services integration projects*. Vol. 1. SRS 76–02012. Washington, D.C.: Author.

Urban and Rural Systems Associates. 1977. *Provider services network project, Draft final report*. San Jose, Calif.: Santa Clara County Office of Education. ERIC Document Reproduction Service No. ED 148 484.

Vander Schie, A. R., M. O. Wagenfeld, and B. L. Worgess. 1987. Reorganizing human services at the local level: The Kalamazoo County experience. *New England Journal of Human Services* 7:31–33.

Vasey, W. 1958. *Government and social welfare*. New York: Henry Holt.

Warren, R. L. 1967. The interorganizational field as a focus for investigation. *Administrative Sciences Quarterly* 12, December:396–419.

Weatherly, R. A., M. H. Levine, S. B. Perlman, and L. V. Klerman. 1987. National problems, local solutions: Comprehensive services for pregnant and parenting adolescents. *Youth and Society* 19 (1): 73–92.

Weissbourd, B. 1987. A brief history of family support programs. In S. L. Kagan, D. Powell, B. Weissbourd, and E. Zigler (eds.), *America's family support programs*. New Haven, Conn.: Yale University Press.

White, O., and B. Gates. 1974. Statistical theory and equity in the delivery of social services. *Public Administration Review* 34:43–51.

Worthy, J. C. 1950. Organizational structure and employee morale. *American Sociological Review* 15:169–79.

Wright, D. S. 1978. *Understanding intergovernmental relations: Public policy and participants' perspectives in local, state and national governments*. North Scituate, Mass.: Duxbury Press.

Yessian, M. R. 1991. *Services integration: A twenty-year retrospective*. Washington, D.C.: Department of Health and Human Services, Office of the Inspector General.

Zimmerman, J. F. 1983. *State-local relations: A partnership approach*. New York: Praeger.

Index

Index   **219**

Education, 74–79; early, 63–71. *See also* Schools; Special education

Education for All Handicapped Children Act (1975), 72

Education of the Handicapped Act Amendments (1986), 74–75

Effectiveness, definition of, 86

Efficiency, 5–6, 9, 86–87, 147, 164

Eisenhower, Dwight D., 12

Elder, J. O., 72

Elected officials, 22, 44, 73; and accountability, 34, 151; budget concerns of, 132, 151, 190; and policy process, 105; and redistribution of income, 24–25; turnover in, 130, 151. *See also* Governors; Leadership; Politics

Elementary and Secondary Education Act (ESEA), 14, 51, 66, 77

Eligibility requirements, 4, 97, 127, 133, 184, 195–96

Employment services, 11, 17

EPSDT. *See* Early and Periodic Screening, Diagnosis and Treatment

Family: as barrier to children's services, 63–64

Family Resource and Youth Service Centers (Ky.), 152

Family support programs, 38, 61–62, 91, 107, 182

Farrow, F., 133

Federal Assistance Streamlining Task Force (FAST), 31

Federal Emergency Relief Agency, 65

Federal government, 11; and child care, 63–67, 71–75; as guarantor of reform, 10, 48, 181; role of, in providing services, 6, 10–16, 23–24, 133–34; and service integration, 28–54, 71–75, 165–66, 181–82; and state governments, 11–14, 23, 49, 64, 165.

See also Federalism; Intergovernmental relations; *Names of departments of the federal government*

Federalism: Cooperative, 13, 15, 101; Coordinated, 14; Creative, 15, 18–22, 41, 101; Dual, 13, 15; "New," 22–25, 28, 41, 90, 101, 165; "reform" of, under Reagan, 52–53; and replication of reforms, 171; and service integration, 3–5, 11, 100–101, 165

Federal Panel on Early Childhood, 68

Federal Security Agency, 11, 12. *See also* Department of Health, Education and Welfare

Federal Works Administration, 65

Feeder Bill (1971), 42–45, 46

Feild, T., 172

Fessler, J. W., 98, 99–100

Firestone, W. A., 129, 130, 134

Fishman, M. E., 39

Flintrop, D., 62

Florida, 24, 38, 146, 155, 156

Food stamp legislation, 14, 15

Foundations, 26, 59, 61, 62, 166, 193

4C program, 41, 68

Functionalism, 98–100, 102, 107–8, 109

Funding: for Allied Services Acts, 47–49; as barrier to service integration, 127, 128, 133–34, 173–74; coordination of, 148–50; flexibility in, 30, 45, 46, 50, 51, 53, 153; lack of, as motivation for service integration, 73, 130, 152; need for inventive, 59, 152–53, 192; for service integration, 152–53, 173–74, 176–77; and SIPP, 38; strategies of, 152–53. *See also* Costs

Gaebler, T., 86

Gans, S. P., 142, 187; on integrated

Index

Public institutions, 9–10, 64. *See also* Schools; Segregation
Public-private partnerships, 15, 34, 47, 49, 58–59, 181–82, 193–95
Public sector. *See* Child welfare system; Federal government; Federalism; Local government; Public-private partnerships; State government

Radcliffe-Brown, A. R., 107
Radin, B. A., 54, 167, 175, 177, 183
Rand Corporation, 32–33
Reagan, Ronald, 25–26, 37, 52–53
Reconstruction, 8
Redburn, F. S., 51, 89, 113–14
Redistribution: of wealth, 11, 24
Refinancing, 152–53
Reform. *See* Civil rights movement; Reformers; Service integration; System reform
Reformers, 6, 7–10, 76
Regulations, 48, 50, 62, 127–28, 134, 190
Rein, M., 5, 84–85
Religious institutions, 5, 17
Research and demonstration projects: in categorical programs, 59, 61, 78–79; for federal service integration, 28–35, 42, 49–50, 124–25, 194
Research and Development Task Force, 30
Research Group, 48, 50, 121, 134–36
Richardson, Elliot L., 29–30, 42–44, 47, 51, 58, 86
Rivera, A., 173
Roosevelt, Franklin D., 65
Rosenblum, S., 173
Rothman, D., 7

Sampson, B. C., 120, 132
Scanlon, J., 170
Schlenger, W. E., 57

Schmidt, R., 170
Schools: attempts to promote coordination by, 75–79, 116, 152; and child care programs, 70–71; lack of clarity about purposes of, 84; lack of coordination by, 49, 73, 75, 176. *See also* Education; Special education
Schorr, L., 170
SEAS. *See* State Education Agencies
Segregation: in government programs, 64–65, 67; of handicapped children, 71–72; of poor, 6, 7, 65, 67, 70
Self-sufficiency, 37
Senate Subcommittee on Intergovernmental Relations, 18
Service delivery. *See* Delivery
Service integration: assumptions about, 161–78; barriers to, 34, 35, 124–36, 161–78; changes in conceptions of, 180–86; conceptual frameworks of, 113–23; concerns about, 31, 79, 175–78; costs of, 33, 129–30, 152, 173–74, 184, 190; definitions of, 23, 87–90, 187–89; evaluating outcomes of, 169–74, 185, 190, 192–93; facilitators of, 136–37; federal efforts to achieve, 28–54, 71–75, 165–66, 181–82; findings concerning, 20–21, 25, 32–39, 78–79, 99–100, 117–18, 147; goals of, 9, 17–18, 32, 52–53, 164–65, 175, 187, 188; history of, 3–79, 71, 175; lack of resources a motivation for, 73, 130, 152; multidisciplinary perspective of, 18–19, 55, 196–97; rationales for, 84–87; recommendations concerning, 186–98; strategies for achieving, 26, 106, 138–57, 168–69, 187–88; theories of, 95–110, 113–14, 189–90. *See also* Clients; Delivery; Domains; Professionals; Research and demonstration projects; System reform